A BEAUTIFUL,
TERRIBLE THING

JEN WAITE

A BEAUTIFUL, TERRIBLE THING

A MEMOIR OF MARRIAGE AND BETRAYAL

PLUME

An imprint of Penguin Random House LLC
375 Hudson Street
New York, New York 10014

Plume is a registered trademark and its colophon is a trademark of Penguin Random House LLC.

Library of Congress Cataloging-in-Publication Data
has been applied for.

ISBN: 9780735216464 (hardcover)
ISBN: 9780735216518 (paperback)
ISBN: 9780525533177 (Canadian Edition)

Printed in the United States of America
10 9 8 7 6 5 4 3 2 1

To V.

Everything. Everything. Everything. Is for you.

But out of the mouth of the Mother of God
I have seen the truth like fire,
This—that the sky grows darker yet
And the sea rises higher.

—G. K. Chesterton, *The Ballad of the White Horse*

A Note from the Author

THIS is my personal, lived experience. *Psychopath* and *socio-path* are terms commonly used for someone on the spectrum of antisocial personality disorders. While I made several discoveries based on my intimate experience and observations, I am not a mental-health professional and this is not a clinical diagnosis of psychopathy.

THE air pulses. As I'm staring at the computer, the computer I share with my husband, and holding our screaming three-week-old baby on my lap, my stomach tightens. I read the first line of the e-mail and bile begins to rise into my throat. I try to take a breath, but I can't get any air in. I have to breathe. And I have to make this baby stop screaming. What I am seeing must have a logical explanation. It must be a misunderstanding. As soon as I can talk to my husband, he will explain and everything will be OK. This is not an emergency yet. If I can just hear his voice, I will be able to breathe again. Balancing the baby in one arm, I reach for my cell phone with the other, unconsciously bouncing my knees to soothe my daughter's screams.

BEFORE

MARCO. This man, I knew in my gut, was *it*. I finally understood what it meant, when you "just know." I just knew about Marco. I met him at the Square, the restaurant where we both worked. I got a job as a waitress to make the money that did not seem to be materializing from my acting and modeling careers. Two years out of college, I had quit my job as an analyst at a hedge fund and decided to become a full-time actor, to "go for it." It sounded great in theory.

A year later, I'd gone to audition after audition, casting after casting, and the biggest job I had booked was starring in a holiday vodka commercial. The role called for "blonde, pretty, aspirational, Swedish-looking." Check, and apparently check, check, check. A whole twenty seconds of staring dreamily into the eyes of the chiseled-faced man I had met a few hours before and clinking my glass against his. Having a restaurant job to pay the bills made me a cliché, but it was necessary, and besides, it gave the days structure.

On the first day of training at the Square, a trendy burger restaurant a few blocks from my apartment, I sat with ten other new employees around a large, circular table, listening to Bruce, the tiny, energetic manager, go over the corporate "steps of service." It was my second waitressing job—the first, a chain restaurant in midtown (the only place that would hire me with no experience) lasted just two months. As Bruce danced around the restaurant, demonstrating when to bring steak knives versus butter knives to a table, I scanned the faces around the table, landing on dark brown eyes belonging to one of the bartenders. He was tall and Latin with black, slicked-back hair and mocha skin. Judging by his accent when he asked a question about the bar setup a few moments earlier, he had been born elsewhere but had lived in the States awhile; the way he spoke was confident and fluid. Our eyes briefly locked, and he gave a quick, easy smile. I looked away, willing myself not to blush. I had learned long ago that the best way to survive in New York City was to keep my defenses up at all times. And anyway, I was happy with my long-distance boyfriend back home in Maine. Jeff had light blue eyes, curly brown hair, and a build comprised of the muscles he used every day in his construction job. When I saw him without clothes, it was like seeing a Greek god in the flesh. I had never seen a body like that in real life before. I had met Jeff while I was home for the summer helping my mom recover from surgery. When I went back to New York at the end of the summer, we substituted drunken nights on his couch for hours on the phone, and what was supposed to be a fun fling somehow turned into a yearlong romance. Our relationship of texting and sporadic weekend visits was easy, and he made me laugh.

The meeting ended, and I gathered my notebook and pen and slid my sunglasses up to rest on top of my head. I was almost through the doors leading to the street before anyone else had even gotten up from the table. I felt someone come up right behind me, and suddenly the door was opening. It was the Latin.

"Jen, right?" Except the way he said it, it sounded like "Gin."

"Um, right. Sorry, I was just—"

"I'm Marco, the bar manager. Bruce asked me to hand out these employee packets to everyone at the end of the meeting, but you ran away before I could give you one," he said, passing me some rolled-up sheets of paper.

"Oh, sorry, I was just . . . thanks." I couldn't help but meet his open face with a smile.

"Well, you're obviously in a hurry," he said with a wink, and then walked away before I could respond.

The next day at work we did speed drills at the bar to see how quickly the bartenders could churn out drinks during a rush.

"Send three drinks on different tickets, right now, *bam, bam, bam*," Bruce whispered to me, and rubbed his hands together. I put in the order for three drinks.

"Ah, a jalapeño margarita for . . . Gin," Marco said as he read the first bar ticket. My face flushed with color. The next ticket printed. "And a mojito for . . . Gin," Marco said with a half smile. I smiled back as the third ticket printed. "Martini straight up with a twist. Wait. Don't tell me." He scrunched his face up. "For Gin!"

"I'm sorry." I laughed, walking over to the bar. "Bruce made me," I whispered when I got close enough.

"Don't be sorry," he said. "At least I have something nice to look at while I make these drinks."

"Oh. Ha," I said, and forced myself to breathe in and out steadily through my nose.

On the last night of training, before the restaurant opened to the friends and family of the owners the next day, everyone decided to go for a drink at the dive bar two blocks away. I finished my side work and walked to the bathroom to change out of my black uniform.

"Are you coming to Doyle's, Gin?"

I looked up to see Marco walking toward me with his small work duffel bag in hand.

"Umm . . . yeah. I just have to change."

"I'll wait for you at the bar. Everyone else already left," he said with a smile.

"Oh, OK . . . I'll be right out." My heart pounded as I quickly pulled on jeans and a loose T-shirt.

I walked back through the main room of the restaurant. Marco was waiting by the big glass doors.

"After you." Marco held the door open, and we walked through.

"Who said chivalry is dead," I said with a small smile.

"Oh, that's my Latin charm. It's been bred into me over generations and generations," he said seriously.

"Oh, really, is that so?" When our shoulders touched for an instant on the way to Doyle's, I momentarily stopped breathing.

At the bar, we settled in with our coworkers. I sat down next to Andrew, a server with a gleaming bald head and oversize bright white teeth, who immediately began telling me about his relationship troubles with his current boyfriend. Marco ordered two vodka sodas and placed one in front of me. "Double vodka soda for Gin." His smile swept over me. As he walked to the other side of the table, I thought, *I am going to marry that man*. It was a quick, involuntary thought, and I recoiled as soon as it had passed through my mind. I took a long drink through the straw in front of me and focused on the cool liquid sliding down my throat.

For the next hour I talked and joked with Andrew and Karly, a tall, blonde waitress. I'd always thought Karly was icy, but after two beers she melted into a sweet, goofy girl from California. Karly confessed she put on a "bitch face" to fend off advances from the bussers who seemed particularly drawn to her even though she hovered almost a foot above them. I was aware of Marco sitting across the small table from me the entire time, and even though we were both involved in separate conversations, I felt myself speaking every word and making each gesture only for him. As the double vodka soda settled into my bones, loosening my limbs and flushing my cheeks, I pressed my knee into his under the table. For half a second, there was nothing. And then I felt it. A slight returned pressure. Neither of us acknowledged what was happening under the table, and it went unnoticed by all our coworkers.

When everyone else said their good-byes around 2:00 A.M., I turned to Marco and said, "Are you sure you ordered me a double? It was a little weak." Instead of leaving with the others, he grinned and made his way to the bar, saying, "In that case, I better get you another drink or you'll leave dissatisfied, and we wouldn't want that." Karly paused at the door and asked, "Are y'all coming?"

"No, we're gonna have one more. See you tomorrow!"

Pull up, a voice whispered in my head. Instead, I took a large gulp of the drink Marco had just set in front of me.

He wanted to know everything about me. There was something

about the way Marco looked at me; his eyes were so intense, like I was the only person in the bar. I told him about growing up in a small town on the coast of Maine. My childhood filled with sandy beaches and freezing-cold water that gave me ice-cream headaches when I dunked (but I always dunked anyway) and playing tag at night with the neighborhood kids. I told him about my parents. How they were the parents that my friends wished were their own parents: affectionate, warm, and funny but also just strict enough. My mom worked her way up the corporate ladder as a manager at L.L.Bean, and my dad was a computer engineer. I told Marco about the moment my dad announced that he had quit his job to start his own company. How, even as an eleven-year-old, I knew it was something special and something to be proud of, but the uncertainty made me nervous. After his first two start-ups failed, we saw less and less of him as he worked longer and longer hours. My mom started getting migraine headaches. There was a tension in our house that had never been there before. And then, after four years and three failed start-ups, my parents brought my sister and me into the dining room and told us to look at the newspaper lying on the kitchen table. The tiny little blurb circled in pen read, "CIMA-RON SNAPPED UP BY AMCC." My sister and I shrieked in delight. My father's start-up had been bought by a larger company—we were never told the details, but after that morning, the tension in our house dissipated.

I'm not usually in the habit of revealing much about my childhood, but when Marco looked at me, he saw me, who I really was, and my self-consciousness evaporated. His questions came one after another, and, when I got to the part about my long-distance boyfriend, I blushed but plowed on. Marco just smiled and started talking. He told me about growing up in Argentina, about his grandfather's house in the countryside where he would go for the summer and take care of his grandfather's bunnies (only much, much later would he confess that many of those bunnies ended up on their dinner plates), about his trip to the United States with his mother, father, and older sister when he was eighteen. The trip that changed his life. They came for a family vacation after his graduation from military high school. After spending a week in New York City as a tourist who spoke five words of English, he fell in love with the excitement and energy of the city and refused to board the plane back home. It was a split-second decision that resulted in a brand-new life in a foreign country and the most exciting city in the world. Then, five years later, when he was just twenty-three and had worked his way up from a busser, to a server, to a bartender, and had become fluent in English, he got his Polish girlfriend pregnant. The girlfriend broke up with him when the baby was a year old, and he had stayed in New York to be close to his son. He had begged her to try to make it work for their new family, but she had already moved on to someone else. She gave him a week to get out of their apartment so her new boyfriend could move in. That had been seven years earlier.

"I've never told anyone those details before," he said slowly, looking up from his hands.

"I'm so sorry. That's . . ." I reached out and touched his arm.

I wanted to know everything about him, but in the next moment, he cleared his throat and smiled. "I think they're closing up. You better finish your drink."

I leaned forward to take in the last of my vodka soda through the straw.

"Don't do that."

"Do what?" I asked.

"Lean over like that."

I looked down to see cleavage, a lot of cleavage. "On that note . . . it's probably time for me to go home."

Marco walked me home, and we hugged in front of my building. When our bodies pressed together, electricity coursed through my body.

"Well, I think you better go inside right now," Marco said with a laugh. "Because if you don't get out of my sight soon, I might try to kiss you. And I don't want to embarrass myself."

My cheeks flushed with pleasure.

"Good night, Marco."

"Good night, Gin."

AFTER

LOUISA'S screams fill my ears and penetrate the deep recesses of my brain where my decision-making neurons lie. My mind, usually quick and sharp, now feels vast and hollow. I have trouble thinking a single thought clearly. My phone is still in my hand; Lulu is still cradled in the other arm. I scroll through my recent calls and find "Mi Amor," but before I hit call my brain jolts back into action. I place my phone on the coffee table. I look at the e-mail again. It is dated almost two weeks ago, January 9. Two weeks ago I was in Maine with Lulu and my parents in my childhood home. Marco's boss was taking vacation the first couple of weeks of January, and Marco was going to be working nonstop at Angel's Wing, the trendy downtown restaurant he manages.

"Baby, you should go home to Maine with Louisa. I'll barely be able to help you, and I'll feel terrible knowing you're doing everything alone." And I'd thought, *My sweet, workaholic husband, he's going to make himself sick trying to provide for us.* I was proud that my husband wanted to give his family everything, even if he had to work fourteen-hour days. That morning, January 1, when I left with Lulu for Maine, I kissed Marco good-bye and started to cry as our lips met.

"Baby, don't cry; you'll be back soon. Please don't cry," he said.

I gasped out between sobs, "I know, I know. I'm sorry. It's just hormones. I love you so."

"I love you, too. So much."

I couldn't explain in that moment that sometimes, out of no-where, my love for him filled me up and overflowed my body, and it had nothing to do with hormones. That sometimes I would have dreams that I had lost him. I would wake up with a start, relief flooding my body as I felt him beside me and then memorized the freckle under his eye as he snored softly. That the reason I started saying "I love you so" to him years ago was because I couldn't fit all that love into the word *much*.

This is the first time in the three weeks since Louisa was born that I have opened a computer. I look back at the e-mail. My eyes flick up to today's date in the top, right corner of the screen. January 20. I clumsily move the mouse up to the subject line of the e-mail. "Appointment," it reads. Marco has forwarded the e-mail to someone—a woman. The sick feeling in my stomach is growing and twisting, and there is still a disconnect in my brain; the neu-rons are sitting complacently, glancing at one another nervously instead of connecting and dancing like they usually do. Through my brain fog, I manage to bring up Facebook. With my free hand, I type the foreign letters of the name into the search bar: V-I-K-T-O-R-I-J-A. I tap the last letter, and a profile pops up. One mutual friend. My husband. This is not good.

BEFORE

I HAD the next day off from work, and I spent the morning getting ready for the three auditions I had that afternoon. One was for a pet-food commercial, one was for an off-off-Broadway play, and one was two lines on a prime-time television show (two lines!). All called for completely different wardrobes and looks. By the time I had packed the clothes, shoes, and makeup I would need for the day, my backpack was bursting at the zipper. All three auditions went fine. Not bad, not amazing, just fine. Somehow they were all over before I even realized they were happening. I left each casting room with a sinking feeling. The chipper "Thank you's" from the casting directors really seemed to say, "I won't remember you five seconds from now, but thanks for wasting everyone's time." I walked to the train from my last audition thinking about everything I should have done in the audition room that I hadn't. The buzz of my phone brought me back to the sidewalk.

"Drink at Doyle's?"

My heart sped up, and all thoughts of my failed auditions floated away as I imagined seeing Marco again. It was 4:30 P.M. It seemed early for a drink, but the thought of being in a dark, cool bar that smelled of old beer and peanuts was deliciously freeing. I had no obligations, nowhere to be, and no one to answer to. Except Jeff. *Just one drink,* I told myself. *There's nothing wrong with one drink with a coworker.* I responded, "Meet you in 30," and sped down the subway steps to catch the train pulling into the station.

Marco was wearing a black T-shirt that showed off lean, muscular arms. Black ink formed a tattoo on his forearm, and I saw that it was a Nietzsche quote: "And when you gaze long into an abyss, the abyss also gazes into you." He was sexy and mysterious and all of a sudden I wanted him more than I had wanted anything in my life. I sat down on the bar stool next to him and ran my finger along his tattoo.

"Pretty dark," I said.

"I got it when I was twenty-five and my son's mom had just left me. I decided right then and there that I wouldn't ever try to find happiness again."

He told me that after Seb's mom, Natalia, had left him, he had rebounded immediately with another Eastern European girl, Tania, a hostess where he worked at the time. He told Tania that he was still in love with someone else and that he wasn't ready for a serious relationship, but somehow they had stayed together for seven years. It was a miserable seven years, full of fighting and distrust. I asked him why on earth they had stayed together for so long, and he said their relationship was a crutch for both of them;

neither were happy but both were afraid to let go and have nothing. They had finally broken up a few months earlier. He dropped my gaze. "There's something I have to tell you," he said.

"Yes?" I tapped my foot rhythmically under the table and then clamped my hands down on my knees. *I knew it. He has a girlfriend,* I thought, and then reminded myself, *and you have a boyfriend.*

"I'm not legal. I've been living in the States for twelve years illegally. I can't go home and visit my family. I can't get a job that isn't willing to pay me under the table. My grandma died a few months ago, and I couldn't go to the funeral or say good-bye. . . ." His voice broke and trailed off. We were both quiet for a moment as I struggled to find the right words. He pulled his chair closer to the table so that his knee brushed mine. "You know . . . I hadn't allowed myself to be hopeful about ever being happy again until I met you." He looked at me with such a combination of intense sadness and awe that my head felt light and fuzzy.

Suddenly, I was leaning toward him. His hand brushed the side of my face as our lips touched and opened, and my heart pounded as our mouths and tongues came together and explored each other. It was a kiss unlike any other in my life. For twenty seconds I was transported to a completely different world where only Marco existed. When I pulled away from him, finally aware that we were still in a dive bar and the bartender was a mere twenty feet away, his eyes searched my face, and he tucked a strand of hair behind my ear.

"Wow." The word came out of his mouth in a low sigh.

"Do you want to come back to my apartment?" I asked quickly.

What the hell are you doing? the voice in my head yelled.

Back at my apartment, I led Marco into my bedroom. When he laid me down on my bed and then slowly unbuttoned my shirt, kissing my neck, my breasts, my stomach, I started to cry. He intertwined my fingers with his. "I can stop," he whispered, and I nodded, unable to speak, embarrassed that I turned out to be a fraud, not the exciting, adventurous "bad" girl I thought I could be. He climbed up beside me and kissed me sweetly, wiping away my tears with his thumb.

"I'm sorry, I feel like such an idiot," I mumbled. "I thought I could do this but . . . I've never cheated and—"

"It's OK. You don't have to be sorry." He kissed me again and laid his hand on my waist. The kiss grew more intense. This time it was me reaching down to undo his belt. I was in control, and my apprehension was replaced by courage. I pulled him on top of me and guided him inside me, his eyes locked with mine the entire time. When it was over, there was no awkwardness or disappointment that usually rushed in after the first time with someone new. We laid side by side looking at each other, and I thought, *I have to break up with Jeff.*

A half hour later, right as Marco was about to leave, our good-bye kiss turned into him pressing me against the wall, and as it grew more intense, he spun me around and pulled down both our jeans, thrusting inside me as I bit my lip, half ecstatic, half nervous about my roommate coming home any minute. After he finally left, I staggered back to my bedroom in a daze and started to cry again as reality rushed back in.

The next few days passed in a blur. I thought about Marco nonstop. I broke up with Jeff the next time he came to visit. When I told him that the distance was just too much, that we had different priorities, what I really meant was: "I've met someone else, and I've already moved on." I cried because he cried, but it was like ripping off a Band-Aid—painful for a moment and then just a slight stinging that faded into the background.

I practically skipped to work the days I knew I would be working together with Marco. One morning, I walked into work and immediately checked the schedule posted in the changing area. Marco would be coming in in a few hours! I changed quickly into my black shirt and pants, smiling and humming the whole time.

"Um, you're in a good mood. Did you get laid last night?" Andrew asked as he sashayed into the locker room.

"No, I'm just a happy person. Not everyone can have perfect resting bitch face like you and Karly," I said with a smile.

"Oh, wait, right I forgot you're from Maine. Everyone from Maine is happy. Just wait until you've been in New York longer. You'll see. There will be a lot less humming and smiling and a lot more 'step off or I will cut you, bitch.'"

I laughed. "I can only hope. I am learning from the best."

"Damn straight, honey," he said, and pushed back through the swinging doors into the main dining room.

A few hours later, I sidled up to the bar as Marco was settling in for his shift.

"Oh, hi," he said. "I didn't know you were working today."

"I'm on a double," I said.

"Oh no," he said, smiling, and then dropped his voice, "this is really bad."

"What?" I asked, looking around.

"Every time I see you, I get really, really happy," he said. "What are you doing to me?"

Before I could respond, Bruce walked by and Marco said louder than he needed to, "Jen, could you help me get a keg from the walk-in? The nut brown ale is tapped."

"Do you want me to grab one of the guys to help you?" Bruce said as he breezed by.

"Oh no," I said quickly. "It's OK. I'm stronger than I look."

As we walked through the kitchen to the walk-in refrigerator, I whispered, "Is the nut brown really tapped?"

"Maybe. Maybe not," Marco said with a grin.

He closed the huge refrigerator door behind us and turned toward me, placing one hand on my waist. "Hi," he said.

"Hi."

"Do you know how extremely beautiful you are?" he asked, tugging a strand of hair behind my shoulder.

"Do you know how extremely cheesy you are?" I said, laughing, aware of his thumb rubbing my side and the closeness of his chest to my body.

"Oh, that's my Latin charm," he said.

I wondered if he could feel my heart pounding a few inches away.

He cocked his head, and then his other hand was cupping my chin and he was drawing me in for a long, intense kiss. "I think I could kiss you all day," he said. My heart beat harder. "But unfortunately people might start to wonder where we are."

"And we would get really cold," I said.

"I would keep you warm," he said with a wink.

"I better get back to my tables," I said, and started toward the door.

"Hey, I still need your help with the keg."

"I thought that was a ploy," I said.

"Nope. I was just mixing business with pleasure."

———

OVER the next few weeks, I spent every second thinking about Marco. Whenever we were together, I felt the tiniest bit drunk. I had a strange sensation of seeing the world in color for the first time—after not even knowing I was living in black and white before. We texted hundreds of times a day; every morning I woke up to a rush of endorphins as I read Marco's messages: "Good morning, beautiful," "Time to wake up, sexy," "How do you make me so happy?" At work we were like lovestruck teenagers, trying our best to act blasé around each other in front of coworkers and failing miserably. We met in the locker room and exchanged salty, hot kisses, made even more exciting and furious by the fact that someone could walk in at any time. We went to Doyle's with our coworkers most nights and always stayed for "one more drink." After everyone else had left the bar, Marco would pull his chair closer to me and drag his finger across my neck, telling me about his dream to open his own bar someday. And I told him how scared I was that I was going to fail, like so many others, at acting, but that it was the only thing that I wanted to do.

Except that was no longer true. I wanted to be with Marco. I wanted it to be my full-time occupation. It didn't matter where we were or what we were doing; I just wanted to be close to him, forever.

In late September, he announced that his sister, Sofia, who lived in Denmark with her investment-banker husband, had had her first baby, a boy named Domenico. He asked me to come with him to pick out a baby gift, and we met at Bloomingdale's on a beautiful, sparkling afternoon. With Marco's arm draped around my shoulders, we took the escalator up to the baby-clothes section. We walked through the racks slowly, touching fifty-dollar onesies, running our fingers along silk baby kimonos, picking up a four-hundred-dollar baby bathing suit with a frilly pink tutu, and laughing. The expensive department store air, the way Marco leaned down to kiss my neck, the adorable newness of the baby clothes—all of it mixed together into a cocktail that made me feel woozier than any double vodka soda. After asking my opinion about the tiny shirts, Marco settled on a miniature white T-shirt with a blue outline of the Manhattan skyline on the front, perfectly touristy and elegant for his new nephew.

On our way back down to the first floor, Marco pulled me off the elevator and led me to Forty Carrots, where he ordered a small frozen yogurt topped with peanut butter cups to share. The no-nonsense yogurt lady handed us an overflowing cup of yogurt—white waves and ripples punctuated by heaps of brown chocolate and peanut butter.

"This may be the best thing I've ever tasted," I said as Marco spooned a bite into my mouth.

"I thought you might like it," he replied, digging back into the cup and bringing another overflowing spoonful into my mouth. After my third bite, I told him he had to try it.

"Oh no, I hate peanut butter," he said, smiling.

"What? Why did you order peanut butter cups then?" I asked.

"You mentioned once that they're your favorite candy."

Marco watched me eat with a glowing satisfaction.

"See. It was worth not taking a bite, just to watch how happy that made you," he said, and brought my fingers to his mouth, swirling his tongue around my pointer finger and then licking away the stickiness from the rest of my fingers. "I don't think I'll ever be able to get enough of you," he said, pulling me against him so tight that I felt his excitement growing. I thought, *I know exactly what you mean.*

AFTER

"MAY I speak to Marco, please?" I ask politely, keeping my voice as steady as possible even though it comes out high-pitched and slightly wobbly. The hostess says, "Just one moment." While I wait, my eyes travel back to the e-mail. *My girlfriend and I have decided to go with another apartment, but thank you for your time.* Girlfriend, girlfriend, girlfriend. Why is my husband calling me his girlfriend? And what apartment? I study the profile picture that fills the other half of the screen. A blonde woman in a fur coat stares back at me. She is wearing large black sunglasses perched on the tip of her nose. Her glossed lips are pursed into a duckface. Long, blonde hair falls straight to her waist. Viktorija Novak.

"This is Marco." My husband's voice fills my ear, strong, assertive, work-mode Marco.

"*You're having an affair,*" I scream. Beside me, Louisa erupts in an equally impressive scream. I hold my breath. I've almost never raised my voice at my husband in the five years we've been together. We never fight. We've always just gotten along; the few fights we've had, we've always been able to resolve with some deep breaths and calm discussion. Part of me is already thinking how we will make this into a joke, after he explains everything, after the miscommunication is cleared up. It will be our "crazy, first few weeks postbaby" fight, over some ridiculous misunderstanding. *So she actually thought I was having an affair with a fur-coat-wearing club girl right after Louisa was born,* I imagine him telling our friends. Everyone will laugh at the absurdity of Marco—*Marco,* the guy who gets made fun of on a regular basis for how unapologetically obsessed he is with me— having an affair. But another part of me, the deep-down, behind-the-walls-of-my-stomach part of me, sits with the phone pressed hard against my ear, not breathing, waiting for something in his voice to tell me everything I need to know.

"Babe," he says calmly, "what are you talking about?"

"I found an e-mail"—the words come out in a rush—"between you and an apartment broker and you say 'my girlfriend.' What the hell is going on, Marco?"

He laughs. A goofy, genuine, incredulous laugh, and it is the sweetest thing I have ever heard, because in that laugh I know that this is exactly what I thought: a misunderstanding. Now he will explain and everything will be OK.

"Baby, first of all, trust me when I say I am not having an affair. I would never, ever cheat on you. You are my life. Baby? I want you to hear that. You are my life, OK?"

"OK," I say, and all the muscles I didn't realize I was holding tight loosen back into their normal spots. I breathe again because I know this is true.

"Second, this is all a mix-up, and you're seriously going to laugh when I tell you. This server, she's Croatian, and she's new in the States. She saw me looking at apartments for us on my office computer and she pleaded with me to call the broker for her. She has no savings and no credit and no broker will take her seriously when she calls them." His voice is calm and steady. "Now that I'm thinking about it from your perspective, it was really stupid of me to say 'my girlfriend' when I wrote, but I was really trying to help and get some appointments set up for her so she has somewhere to live. I am so, so sorry, babe. I'm an idiot."

"OK," I say again. I know he is telling the truth, I feel it in my bones, but I am still shaking. "That's really fucking inappropriate to call someone else 'my girlfriend.'"

"I know, I know, I am realizing that now, and I'm so sorry. Please don't cry. It's really all a stupid mistake."

"I need you to come home now, Marco. I believe you, but I am having a really hard time with this. You crossed a major line when you did this kind of favor for another woman. I don't care how innocent it may have been. It makes me feel so extremely uncomfortable. We need to talk about this in person."

"OK." I can tell he hears the seriousness in my voice. "I'm coming home; just let me tie up some loose ends here first. I'll be home in an hour, OK?"

I don't say anything. An hour seems like an eternity. Louisa is now screaming so hard she has begun to choke on her screams.

"Babe? OK?"

"OK. I love you."

"I love you so much. I'll be home soon."

Thank God.

BEFORE

"SEBASTIAN, this is Jen. Jen, Seb." Marco nudged the small boy in front of me, and Seb reached out a skinny arm to meet my hand. I was meeting Marco's seven-year-old son for the first time on a hot Saturday afternoon at a tiny Brazilian restaurant a few blocks from my apartment.

"Oops. Oh dear, excuse me," Seb said, pulling his hand back. "Let me just . . . OK, sorry about that." He pocketed the small white object he had been holding and brought his hand back up to mine.

"It's so nice to meet you," I said, settling into a booth across from Marco and Sebastian. "What were you holding?" I asked with a smile.

"Oh." Seb looked at me seriously through thick glasses. "That was a shell I found on the beach at Coney Island. It belonged to some sort of crustacean, though I'm not positive which exactly."

"Ah, how cool," I replied with a side-glance at Marco.

"Crustacean?" I mouthed. Marco smiled back and ruffled his hand through Sebastian's thick, wavy black head of hair. "Seb's in top class at his school."

"Top class? Is that like honors?" I asked.

"They basically take the smartest kids from the entire second grade and shove them into one class together," Seb explained. "I'm learning things that even some third graders don't know."

"Wow, that's awesome." I smiled.

"The only downside is that sometimes I get a whole hour of homework. My mom says it's criminal," Seb said with a sigh, and nibbled on a tortilla chip.

"I agree with your mom," I replied, trying to hide my amusement.

At the end of lunch, Seb turned to me and asked, "Do you want to come play checkers at my dad's apartment?"

"Sure, I would love to." My eyes flicked to Marco. "As long as your dad says it's OK."

"Oh, it's fine," Seb replied quickly. "We don't have any plans, right, Dad?"

"No, we do not," Marco said with a grin. "Except for daddy-son video-game bonding time."

"Oh dear, right, I forgot." Seb drummed his fingers on the table. "We play video games together on the weekends. It's the only time I get to play. My mom doesn't have a PS4 at her house, unfortunately," he told me.

"Ah, I see," I said with a smile. "Well, those sound like very important plans indeed."

"I'm really torn," Seb continued seriously. "Because seventy-five percent of me wants to play checkers with you, but twenty-five percent of me wants to play video games, and I know I'll have regrets if I don't spend as much time as possible gaming this weekend."

"I completely get it. Maybe I can come over another time," I said as we slid out of the booth.

When I hugged Marco good-bye, he whispered into my ear, "He really likes you."

"I really like him," I whispered back, and then wrapped Seb in a hug.

"You should definitely hang out with us again," Seb said. "That was surprisingly fun."

"Well, thank you. I will definitely take you up on that," I said as Marco squeezed my hand behind my back.

A few weeks later, I was invited to Sebastian's eighth birthday party at his mother's apartment. I held on to Marco's hand tightly as we made our way up two flights of stairs to Natalia's apartment. After hearing how she broke Marco's heart, I had prepared myself for a strained first meeting. Instead, I was introduced to a smiling, pretty, petite Polish woman.

"Hi! I'm Natalia, or Nat is what most people call me," she said, giving me a warm kiss on the cheek. "Thank you for spending so much time with my child over the past couple of weeks. Honestly, I don't know how people spend time with other people's children. I can barely stand my own," she said with a laugh. I liked her immediately. After cake and ice cream, she ushered me into her bedroom. "Look, I just wanted to tell you really quickly, thank you. I know it may be soon to say this, but you've really changed our lives."

"What?" I asked. "What do you mean?"

Nat dropped her voice to a whisper. "Marco's ex-girlfriend was a nightmare. Or I should say, they were a nightmare together.

All they did was fight. Marco was always in a terrible mood. Never smiled. Smoked all the time because she smoked. Selfishly"—she paused and ran her hands through long, dark hair—"I'm so, so glad they broke up. Now everything is different. Seb actually wants to hang out with his dad."

I blushed. "It means so much to me that you said that. Sebastian is . . . well, you know. He's incredibly special."

"He is, isn't he?"

———

THE first time I brought Seb home to meet my family, my best friend, Holly, rode with him in the back of my green Subaru. Holly and I grew up next door to each other and both moved to New York after college. In high school, she was chubby and too tall with a curly blonde perm, and she was voted Class Clown our senior year. In college, though, she slimmed down and suddenly her five-feet-ten-inch stature and startling large eyes landed her in a top modeling office in New York City. After her perm was straightened and razored into a chic bob by her agency, her physical transformation was complete. But the girl who won Class Clown still lived in a supermodel's body. "Oh, fuck, I mean, shoot! I'm sorry, buddy," Holly said to Seb as she shook her hand and winced in pain. "The seat-belt thingy broke my nail. Fuck, that hurt. I mean, crap, that hurt. Ugh. Sorry, guys." Seb giggled behind his hand, delighted at this outpouring of cursing from an adult. We were coming home for another close friend's wedding.

Sebastian was eight going on forty-eight, and Holly had dubbed him a "non-Jewish child Woody Allen" after he explained to her exactly why he had no interest in going on roller coasters or

Ferris wheels. ("My idea of fun is not hurtling through the air, feeling like I might throw up, and risking death.") Seb and I had become fast friends after that first lunch. I became enamored of this whip-smart, wiser-than-his-years little adult with a mop of wavy black hair and pale winter skin that turned a gleaming nut brown in the summer. He preferred checkers and computer games to playing sports, reading nonfiction history books to watching TV, and he spoke more eloquently than most adults.

Marco had met my parents several times by then. My parents' opinions mattered to me. If my partner didn't pass the twin tests of my mom's magical intuition and my dad's practical mind, the relationship usually didn't last long. Before meeting Marco, my parents had heard only tidbits about him (six years older, bartender, has a kid), and their hackles were raised. My mom flew to New York City a few months after Marco and I became serious, under the pretense of wanting to have a fun girls' weekend in New York City, but we both knew she was there to vet this choice of partner. In a tiny, cozy bar near Gramercy Park, over a bottle of prosecco and delicious bite-size hors d'oeuvres, Marco and my mom shared stories of completely different but happy childhoods.

"When I was very young, maybe five or six years old, my parents sent me away for the summer to my grandfather's farm in the countryside, a few hours outside of Buenos Aires. My job was to look after the bunnies that my grandfather kept on the farm." Marco paused to fill my mom's glass. "Your glass is only halfway full. That will not do, Maggie."

My mom smiled and lifted her glass. "So did you have a favorite bunny?"

"It was a lot of fun and they were adorable, but I didn't get too attached. They weren't exactly pets, if you know what I mean." Marco popped a Brie-covered crostini into his mouth with a crunch.

My mom's eyes widened. "You mean you ate the bunnies?!"

"Bunny tastes very similar to chicken," Marco responded seriously, and then broke into a huge smile. "I was on a farm in the middle of nowhere in the Argentinian countryside. I did what my grandfather told me."

"That actually reminds me of my childhood summers in Maine," my mom said with a warm smile. "I was a bit older and lobsters aren't quite as cute as bunnies, but I was a lobsterman when I was sixteen."

My mom finished telling Marco about her summer as a lobster fisherman that earned her enough money for an exchange program to Sweden; her first time out of the state of Maine. Whatever reservations my mom came into that bar with trickled away as we drained the bottle of prosecco and laughed and talked, until I looked at my phone and saw that my mom and I were late for our dinner reservation downtown.

"He's *very* charming," my mom said later that night over dinner. "But be careful. He comes with a lot of baggage."

"But, Mom," I exclaimed with the passion of a girl desperately in love, "don't you want me to be with someone who has potential?"

My mom looked at me and said, "You really believe in this guy, huh?"

"I do. I know it sounds crazy, but I just have this *feeling*. I've never felt this way, Mom." I ran through the ex-boyfriend file quickly in my head: There was my college boyfriend, Pete, who smoked a lot of pot and was so sweet, so incredibly eager to please that I once waited fifteen minutes for him to decide between bringing me hot cocoa or tea. There was my boyfriend right out of college, the first boyfriend I lived with, Matt, who was smart and nice and had a good job and who I recoiled from every time he kissed me. And then there was Jeff, the Greek god, who was funny and sexy and told me that if I didn't book a big acting job within six months, I should give up and have babies with him. I had never talked excitedly about any boyfriend, preferring to take the opposite approach—the "I'm not so sure" shrug of my shoulders when asked if this guy was "The One" and changing the topic quickly. I always thought he—The One—was out there; I just didn't know what it was supposed to feel like when I found him. Now I knew. This time, instead of desperately diverting the conversation elsewhere, I had the distinct sensation of being part of a romantic comedy and not being able to control the sappy sound bites pouring out of my mouth.

"Ah. *L'amour.*" My mom sighed with a smile and pushed wavy brown hair behind her ear.

"OK, Mom," I said, in a singsong voice, feigning embarrassment, but in my head I was thinking, *Yes! Yes, this is what real, sing-it-from-the-rooftops, heart-melting love feels like.* I found myself turning the conversation back to Marco again and again.

"And he wants to open a restaurant, and I think he would be amazingly successful because he's worked in the restaurant industry for more than ten years and he's so driven."

"That does sound very exciting. How does he feel about your acting career?" my mom asked while trying to fish a dumpling from the bowl in front of us, first with chopsticks and then with her fingers.

"Oh, he's completely supportive. He always says he knows I am going to be successful. We're really supportive of each other. I kind of feel like we can do anything together," I said in a rush of excitement. "I feel like this is how you and Dad must have felt when you were starting out. I've never known what it feels like to be truly part of a team."

"We have always been each other's biggest fan," my mom said. "That's so important in a relationship and a marriage. Dad and I have always had a vision of what we were trying to do and worked together to accomplish it. Big or small, you hunker down and work toward it together. Respect and teamwork. Because if you're not on the same team, what's the point?"

"I have such enormous respect for Marco," I said, my eyes gleaming. For the rest of the night, I asked my mom questions about her and my dad's marriage and listened in a way that I never had before.

My dad met Marco for the first time a few months later at a hole-in-the-wall Venezuelan restaurant a few blocks from my apartment. I was worried about this encounter for so many different reasons. The yin to my mom's warm and effusive yang, my dad is an extreme type A personality, with an intensity and single-mindedness that served him remarkably well as a provider and executive but could be extremely intimidating, especially for new boyfriends. What I didn't count on was that having spent a portion of his childhood living in Honduras, my dad was fascinated with all things South American. He fired off question after question at Marco, from how to pronounce an entrée on the menu to what he thought about the current political climate in Argentina. By the end of lunch, Marco was sweating profusely and my dad was thrilled. Over the next year my dad and Marco developed a tight bond, texting back and forth nearly every day, switching between

English and Spanish, about everything from Latin foods to Tom Brady's ridiculous fifty-yard passes.

If my parents had any lingering reservations about Marco, they were completely eliminated after meeting Seb. When he hopped out of my green Subaru onto Haven Road, my parents were already almost to the car.

"Sebastian!" my mom cried. "We've heard so much about you!"

"Hi there, how are you, young man?" my dad asked, giving Seb's miniature hand a strong shake.

"Well, it's funny," Seb replied very seriously, adjusting his black-rimmed glasses higher on the bridge of his nose. "I feel nervous but also really happy. Two kind of opposite emotions, which is interesting."

That afternoon my mom took Seb into the woods behind our house to pick blackberries, their two heads bobbing above green-and-brown shrubs, immersed in conversation. The next morning, Seb woke up and said, "I'm going to go explore the woods. Bye," as Marco and I each opened one eye from my childhood bed and smiled.

"He's never been out of the city. He's acting like a real kid," Marco said.

The next day, my dad and Seb played game upon game of checkers while Marco and I slept in. By the end of the week, my dad took me aside: "That boy is very, very special. Marco has done a good job." Finally, my two worlds had merged completely.

AFTER

WHEN Marco walks in the door, I am waiting on the couch. Louisa, mercifully, is sleeping in the bedroom, and I pray she gives me a few minutes of quiet so that we can figure this out and make it go away. I expect Marco to start talking and apologizing right away, but he is quiet and sinks into the chair at the foot of the couch without saying a word.

"Marco . . . ?" I begin, and wait for him to start talking. Still nothing. He looks at the floor. "Marco, what the fuck?" Now I am mad.

"Jen, I told you, the e-mail was nothing, a stupid mistake. I barely even know that person. Seriously, how fucking sick do you think I am? That I would be looking at apartments with some random girl when I've been working so much I haven't even seen Seb in two months?" He holds my gaze.

"OK . . . but still." I begin my rehearsed speech about how that e-mail, no matter what his intentions, was completely inappropriate.

"Wait," he says, cutting me off, "I need to talk to you about something." He speaks slowly and rubs his temple with one hand. "For around a year now, I haven't been happy. I lost all my feelings. I think there's something physically wrong with me. Or . . . I don't know. Like right now, I'm looking at you, and I feel nothing. I feel numb."

I taste salt in my mouth. Tears are running down my face. *I feel nothing?* What is happening? I can't wrap my head around the words that are coming out of my husband's mouth. In the back of my mind, I can still see that e-mail faintly, but it is fading, fading into the distance as I hear my husband say once again, "Jen, I have no feelings."

"What . . . what are you talking about?" I feel like I'm trapped in a bad acid trip. Nothing makes sense. There is something very, very wrong with my husband. He is sitting across from me, it is his body, but he is not my husband. "Marco . . . please." I am pleading now, but I don't know what I am pleading for or why.

"You're telling me you haven't noticed anything over the past year?" His usual sweet, chipper voice is replaced by a monotone, and his eyes are . . . dead.

"We just had a baby. Maybe you're overwhelmed and stressed?" I feel a rush of worry. Is he really hurting? I rack my brain, trying to push past the sludge of hormones and panic and really think about the past year. We finally celebrated our civil ceremony that took place two years ago with a huge reception in Maine, we went to Argentina to visit Marco's family, and we went to France on vacation with my family and Seb. All of these are happy memories—in fact, some of the happiest of my life.

"What are you unhappy about? I don't understand."

"Babe, we barely see each other anymore. I'm always working.

We never do fun couple things anymore. You used to really put effort into your appearance, you know? I mean I would look at you before an audition and think, *Goddamn*."

"But . . ." How do I say this without sounding obvious? "I just had a baby." It comes out in a whisper.

"Oh, I know, I know, that's not what I meant. I just mean, maybe what everyone always says is true, that getting married ruins relationships."

"I don't understand," I say slowly, trying to bide myself time. Maybe if I speak slowly enough and think very, very hard, I will grasp what my husband is saying. "What do you mean, 'getting married ruins relationships'? We're happy. We're so happy." My voice comes out high. I am happily married. I am happily married and in love. I am so in love, and I just had a baby with my husband.

My husband keeps his eyes on the floor and says, "You know men don't like hair down there, right?"

I pull my legs together instinctively and then flinch as the gauzy pad rubs against my swollen flesh. My cheeks burn. "But I couldn't reach during the last few months and now I have stitches." I stumble and stop, unable to form any more words.

"I know," he says quickly. "I'm just saying. . . ." His voice trails off. The buzzing in my ears grows louder and louder.

By now it is close to 2:00 A.M., and Marco says, "I need to get some sleep. Baby, don't worry, we'll figure this out." I am so exhausted and Louisa will be awake soon, but I will never be able to sleep again because my husband has just told me he looks at me and feels nothing. I lie awake, my eyes burning. At 4:00 A.M., Louisa starts to stir with muffled sounds that quickly turn into a full-fledged crying shriek. I pick her up and walk back and forth across the soft carpet of our bedroom. "*Shhhhh, shhhhh, shhhhhh,*" I say, bouncing her in my arms. "*Shhhhhh, shhhhhhh, shhhhhhh.*" But the shushing gets stuck in my throat and my head feels light and heavy at the same time. There is a black tidal wave creeping toward my eyes, and suddenly I am on the carpet, on my knees, holding Louisa straight out in front of me, just above the floor.

"Ah," I hear come out of my mouth from far away. I am on the floor for what seems like an eternity before I hear the groan of the bed and Marco's feet hitting the ground.

"Give her to me," he says. That is all he says. I pass our baby to my husband from my crouched position on the ground and crawl to the bed and hoist myself up. I walk into the living room and sit on the couch, paralyzed. My eyes move slowly back to the computer screen. The e-mail between Marco and the apartment broker stares back at me. I see the name that he has forwarded the e-mail to: Viktorija Novak. I type the name into the search bar at the top of his e-mail, and a dozen e-mails pop onto the screen. I scan them quickly and see they are all work schedule e-mails. Except. What is that? I open up an e-mail with no subject from her to him. Six days ago. It is a link and only the words "*This made me think of you*" in the body of the e-mail. I click the link and in another window up pops an article titled "36 Questions that Can Make Two Strangers Fall in Love."

BEFORE

THE night Marco proposed was the night of my parents' annual Christmas party. Earlier that week we had gone back to the kids' section at Bloomingdale's to buy Sebastian a fancy sweater and nice khaki pants. As I watched my little family wander through the clothing racks, I thought about the difference between infatuation and love.

"Do you remember when we came here to buy Domenico a present?" I asked Marco while holding up a bow tie to Seb.

"What was that . . . two years ago?" he said, lacing his fingers through mine.

"Just about," I said, and then whispered in his ear, "Do you remember how hot for each other we were?"

"Oh, yes," he whispered back, pulling me in for a kiss. "You better watch out, young lady; this old man can still learn tricks that are new."

I smiled to myself at the mangled expression and replied, "Yikes."

That afternoon just as we were descending the slushy steps into the 59th Street subway, Seb perked up. "Hey, guys, wouldn't it be a good idea to get hot cocoa right now? It's been weeks since I've had any."

"Weeks?" Marco replied. "This is a catastrophe. Let's ask Jen what she thinks, though. She might have to get back home." Marco winked at me.

"Hm." I looked at Seb seriously. "You definitely look weak. Like a boy who could use some chocolate, stat."

We reversed direction and took the R train downtown to Union Square. On the walk from the train, we each took one of Seb's hands, pulling him forward against the sharp gusts of icy air.

"Are you sure there's hot chocolate around here?" Seb looked around unconvinced. "My mom and I have been to Union Square before, but we only come here to get me sneakers. I really don't think there's any place that sells hot chocolate."

"Just wait." I smiled into frozen cheeks and pulled our chain toward the brown heavy doors a few steps away. A blast of warm air and the smell of thick, sweet chocolate greeted us.

"Welcome to Max Brenner. Three for lunch?" the hostess said as Seb broke away and walked over to a huge vat of chocolate in the middle of the room. His eyes wandered over the rest of the room, shelves filled with white, milk, and dark chocolate truffles, a table showcasing coarsely chopped hunks of chocolate, burlap bags labeled CACAO, and glass tubes with milk chocolate burbling through.

"Just dessert," Marco replied as Seb whispered, "This is awesome," into the room.

"I think we should definitely do this once a month," I said, unwinding my scarf from my neck and settling into a cushiony chair.

"I second what Jen said." Seb plunked down in the chair between Marco and me. "Maybe I can start staying with you guys a couple days during the week, too? Instead of just the weekends?"

Marco and I looked at each other and then both burst out, "That would be great," at the same time.

"I still need to be with my mom on Tuesdays and Wednesdays because we're in the middle of a *Lost* marathon," Seb said.

"That's fine. We'll figure it out, buddy." Marco reached for my hand across the table, and I squeezed his fingers and took a mental picture of this moment, of my new family.

When Sebastian made his entrance that night at the Christmas party, descending the stairs into the living room from the guest room where he slept upstairs, the ten or so guests who had already arrived oohed and aahed about how handsome he looked, and a neighbor cried, "Lookin' sharp there, young man!" Seb was already a local celebrity among our Maine family and friends, and his reputation of being scarily smart and effortlessly articulate preceded him.

I was sitting on the couch in my parents' living room, talking with Holly and admiring how beautiful this room in particular became every Christmas. The room with its white, plush couches and red shelves filled with impressive-looking hardcover books (that my dad had procured from the town "swap shop") was the perfect setting for the too-big Christmas tree that sparkled with white lights and family ornaments dating back to 1990. Seb sidled up to us with a glass of cranberry juice in hand and patiently waited for Holly to finish her sentence.

". . . and he does this every winter, man. He *hates* being naked and cold. Unless it's the perfect temperature, I get frozen out. We got a space heater because Mama has needs," Holly finished telling me about her computer engineer husband Mike's dislike of having sex when the temperature dropped below freezing. Holly sensed Sebastian standing to the side of her just out of her peripheral vision and swiveled around. "And that is the end of the story I was telling about the dangers of global warming."

Seb took a sip of his cranberry juice. "I've had the-birds-and-the-bees talk with my mom several times by now, you know. I'm nine years old, not two."

"Well excuuuuse me," Holly said, popping a mini crab cake into her mouth.

"Um, Jen, my dad needs to talk to you upstairs about his outfit," Seb said, and I laughed. "OK, I'll be right up." I stood up from the couch and called to Holly as I made my way through the living room, "Marco has better fashion sense than me so this is going to be interesting."

"Can't go wrong with sequined pants," Holly yelled.

I called back, "So helpful."

As I climbed the stairs to my childhood bedroom where Marco and I now stayed on our visits to Maine, I paused to glance at myself in the mirror on the opposite wall. A tomboy at heart, I always dressed up for the family Christmas party. I was wearing a teal fitted dress made of a papery material that hugged my body in all the right places, and my hair hung straight and shiny. I felt glamorous and sexy out of my jeans and T-shirt uniform, and I made a mental note to blow-dry my hair more often. At the top of the stairs I turned left toward the bedroom before seeing that

Marco was standing just to the right of the stairs in a small open room we referred to as "the nook."

"Oh baby, you look great; what are you worried about?" My heart swelled with pride as I took in the tall, dark, and handsome man in front of me (and how cute did he look in a cozy blue sweater with a light-blue collar poking out?!). My face broke into a smile. My boyfriend.

"Jen, babe, I need to ask you something." His voice was oddly formal and shook ever so slightly. The hair on the back of my neck stood up. Oh my God, oh my God. "You know these past couple of years have been the happiest of my life." Oh my God. Now his voice was really shaking, and he took a large gulp of air. "Since I met you, I am excited about the future again, about our future together. Right when I had lost all hope, you've given me a reason to be happy. I feel like we can do anything together." He took a deep breath and reached for both my hands. "Everything has changed for the better. You're like an angel who came into my life, and I can't imagine my life without you. I want to spend the rest of my life with you." Here he reached into his pocket and sank to one knee. "So would you do me the honor of making me the happiest man alive and say you'll marry me?" *Oh my God.*

"Jen? Babe?" I heard Marco's worried voice traveling after me and realized I was walking in circles around the landing, my hands cupping my face.

"Yes," I croaked, walking back to him, still on one knee with a blue velvet box. "Yes, yes, *yes.*" He slipped a simple diamond on my finger, and I screamed and jumped into his arms. "I have never been so sure about anything in my entire life."

Relief flooded his face. "You know you walked away without giving me an answer, right?"

"I did? I think I blacked out." I wrapped my arms around his neck and we kissed and kissed, and then I started laughing hysterically. "I have never been so happy. How did you do it? When did you get the ring? How did you keep this a secret from me?" I peppered him with questions and half listened to his responses as my eyes traveled down to the gleaming stone on my finger.

When we went downstairs my parents were waiting for us with a bottle of champagne and four glasses. "You knew?!" I shrieked, and we toasted.

And my dad said in his booming voice, "Welcome to the family, Marco and Sebastian," and my head swam with happiness. I clinked my glass against Marco's, and my heart felt as if it would burst. My fiancé.

AFTER

I QUESTION Marco about the e-mail with the link to an article about falling in love, and a blank expression comes over his face. "Huh? She never sent me any article.... Oh! Yes, I remember now. She's studying psychology, and she'd been telling me about some experiment involving strangers and questions and falling in love. I pretended to be interested, but I never even read the article. Did you read it? What's it about?" My stomach churns and heaves, but his response is genuine. Earlier this morning, when he found me on the couch looking at her Facebook page, he said, "Jen, Jesus Christ. Just text her if it would make you feel better. This is ridiculous. I told you there is something seriously physically wrong with me, and all you can do is obsess about this random girl?" So I do.

I don't tell Marco, but I bring up the contact he has shared with me (after making sure it matches the number beneath her e-mail signature), and I write: "Hi there. I'm Marco's wife, Jen. We haven't met because I've been really pregnant and then really busy with a newborn baby. I am so embarrassed to be contacting you like this, but I found an e-mail between Marco and an apartment broker about seeing apartments with his girlfriend. He then forwarded the e-mail to you. He has explained it was a misunderstanding, and to be honest, Marco has been the most amazing partner for five years and I know it's crazy not to believe him, but I'm going to blame it on the overload of hormones! Sorry again for this crazy text. Jen."

I put down my phone and then pick it up immediately to see if the text reads "Delivered," and I see the dot-dot-dots of her already typing a reply. I hold the phone inches from my face, waiting for the response. I am paralyzed with fear, and my head feels light with adrenaline. And then:

"Hi Jen. First off, I'm so sorry this has caused you any kind of anxiety or upset. That was not my intention. I have a lot of respect for you as a woman for what you've just been through and congratulations on the birth of your daughter. Marco is telling the truth. He was trying to help me find an apartment and reached out to a broker for me. Men are so stupid sometimes with these things and of course I didn't think twice about it because I just really want an apartment lol. Secondly, I know firsthand that affairs can ruin lives and I would never meddle in a marriage. Once again, I'm really sorry for the misunderstanding. Have a great night."

I shoot off a quick reply thanking her for the response and then turn to Marco. "OK, I'm sorry I was obsessing about the e-mail. I texted Viktorija, and she confirmed that it was a really stupid and inappropriate"—I look at him pointedly—"mistake. So now I'm going to start researching what's going on with you physically. There has got to be some kind of medical explanation. I mean exhaustion, stress. There must be a physical reason why you feel numb." Marco nods and walks slowly to the bathroom. I hear the faucet turn on and then retching from inside. When he comes out he is pale and expressionless, and he mumbles, "I just threw up."

———

AFTER Marco leaves for work that night, I bundle up Louisa and take her around the block in the stroller. I stroll up and down our street as she peers at me through the weather shield. I try to focus on the text message from Viktorija. She confirmed exactly what Marco said. They wouldn't both be lying. But my stomach still lurches and twists, and I have trouble getting air all the way into my lungs. When I pass our apartment for the fifth time, I reach into my coat and take out my cell phone. I call my sister.

"Stella, I need to talk to you about something serious. I haven't told anyone else about this, and I don't think I'm going to. I can't tell Mom and Dad because you know how they are. They'll make a snap judgment and then things will be awkward forever."

"OK. Calm down. What's going on?" I can hear her one-year-old son, my nephew Henry, making unintelligible words in the background and the clattering of plates. I imagine her in a soft oversize sweater, washing lettuce and cradling the phone against her ear, her barely swollen pregnant belly protruding from her otherwise trim frame. I tell her everything except for the article about falling in love. I can't bring myself to disclose that because I know exactly how it sounds. "I'm really confused," I finish. "I don't know what to think."

"Jesus Christ," Stella says. "Well, first of all, that is really inappropriate, even if what he's saying is true, that it was a slip of the tongue and he was doing a favor for someone, that's *still* extremely serious, Jenny."

My stomach drops. "I know. You're right."

"But I also think that's exactly what it was. A stupid, inappropriate flirtation that went a little too far. There's no way that he actually slept with this girl or something. This is Marco we're talking about. His job is to be charming and flirty. And I don't want to upset you even more, but you know I tend to see things in black and white. There's always been a gray area with Marco about what's OK and what's not OK."

"What do you mean?" I ask.

"Remember that Facebook message the first year you guys were dating?"

I had completely forgotten. It was four years ago, an eternity ago, but still, how could I have forgotten? A few months after we became a couple, I saw that he had left his Facebook account up on his computer. I clicked his messages and saw a message he had sent to a girl that read, "Nice profile picture." The profile picture was of her wearing librarian glasses, making a kissy face. She had responded, "Ha-ha my friend took it. You should see the sexy outtakes," and he had written back, "Wanna show me?" The conversation ended there, but I had flipped out. I told him right away I couldn't be in a relationship with him. That I didn't trust him. Marco and I talked for hours and hours about my boundaries versus his boundaries and how we had very different concepts of what was appropriate. He admitted that as a bartender, he was used to flirting for work and maybe he had crossed a line without even realizing it. Finally, he had cupped my face in his hands and said, "Jen, I will never, ever cheat on you. If I ever even come close to feeling dissatisfied with our relationship, I will talk to you. That was the problem in my last relationship; there was no communication. If we're completely open and honest with each other, we can get through anything." And that was when I took a leap of faith. We began to build a real relationship, no longer only based on lust and excitement; slowly but surely we became best friends.

After that incident, nothing had ever happened again. Nat even nudged me a couple of months later and said, "What did you do to Marco? He's really changed. He's blossomed into, like . . . a real man. He's actually mature now."

I had smiled proudly and said, "Yeah? You think?" Part of me was happy it had happened; we had gotten on the same page because of it.

I bring myself back to the conversation with my sister. "Oh, yes, I remember, but, Stella, we talked about that for weeks and nothing like that ever happened again. I mean, that's actually *why* I ended up trusting him, because we had so many discussions about boundaries and trust after that."

"Hmm," she says. "Well, OK, I'm just pointing out that it is now a pattern of behavior. Are you OK with this happening again in, say, five years? Because it seems like this type of behavior is part of who Marco is." Before I can answer she plows on: "But the real issue it seems like is this whole 'I have no feelings' thing."

"Yeah, that really terrifies me. I really do think there is something physical going on."

"Yes, absolutely," Stella says. "Marco works all night and sleeps all day. Do you know how unhealthy it is to never see the sun? I'm sure that there is something seriously wrong with his health. The first thing he should get done is blood work. I'm sure he's critically deficient in vitamin D and a bunch of other things."

My sister's brain works fast and fluidly, like a computer, and her tolerance for bullshit is low.

"Are Rosa and Oscar there yet?" she asks, and I hear the faucet turn on.

Marco's parents planned a big trip to celebrate Oscar's retirement, and their first stop is New York to meet Louisa. They are spending two weeks in my parents' apartment before traveling on to Denmark to spend time with Marco's sister and her family. My parents have found an apartment a few blocks away to sublet for the first three months of Louisa's life. They moved in December 1 and spent the month helping me turn our bedroom into a nursery and waiting for Louisa to make her appearance in the world.

"It's going to be a mishmash of Spanish and English and lots of wine!" my mom had said excitedly a few days ago. A joyous reunion is now seeming unlikely. I push this thought from my mind and say, "Yes, they got in this morning. I haven't talked to them about this yet. The language barrier makes it hard."

"Jenny," she says, "you need to take care of yourself, too. Marco dumped a lot on you. Maybe he really is truly sick and you want to help him, but you just had a baby. You need to do what's right for you and Louisa first."

"OK. Yes. You're right," I say, but all I can think is that Louisa and I need Marco to be OK.

———

I SPEND the next few days madly Googling "numb, no feelings, exhaustion, stress." I finally tell my parents about our talk, but I leave out the part about the e-mail. My mom immediately joins me in trying to find an explanation for Marco's symptoms;

this is her specialty, and she quickly calls me with her theory. "Adrenal fatigue syndrome!" she says excitedly. "Everything I've read matches exactly what Marco is describing. When the human body becomes extremely overtired, the adrenal glands stop functioning, which produces feelings of numbness or loss of feelings." I have no idea what adrenal glands are, but it sounds good.

"Yes, yes, that must be it. Thank God. Mom, thank you, I'm going to start researching now and hopefully we can figure out how to treat it." I hang up and start Googling "adrenal fatigue syndrome," which leads to reading about "medical burnout." By the time I am done reading, I am certain that I've figured out what's wrong with my husband, and I am terrified. For something with a name as innocuous as "burnout," the prognosis is extremely serious, with some individuals who have suffered from the disorder losing their jobs, families, or, even worse, their will to live.

"But this is good," pops into my brain. If it's truly a physical problem, we can figure out the treatment and work through it together. He can get blood work done. Whatever is malfunctioning will show up in tests. According to these websites, it might take months and months of strict rest for him to get better, but what's wrong with him now falls under the category of "something a doctor can fix." The old Marco will come back, and we can be the family that we're supposed to be.

I am about to call Marco at work to tell him what I've found when my eyes travel to the History tab on the screen. I click "show history" and my brain screams, *Stop. Stop. Stop.* But it is too late. I am looking at our Internet history for the past few days. Uber pops up a couple of times; Marco frequently uses the car service to get to and from work, and it has been the subject of tense conversations lately. ("*Babe, your boss should pay for you to take a car if he's keeping you at work till four* A.M. *We're spending a hundred-and-fifty dollars a week on car services; that's ridiculous.*" "*I'll talk to him, but there's no way he's going to pay, baby. It's the restaurant industry; the hours are just really long and late.*") I log into our joint Uber account, not sure exactly what I am looking for and see a list of rides to and from work. I open up a ride from last week at 4:03 A.M. and look at the map that shows the exact route taken from Marco's work in Tribeca to our apartment in Astoria. Except... what is that? There is a stop somewhere in Williamsburg. My heart races. I open up another ride, this one from two nights ago at 5:30 A.M. (Marco got home at 6:10 A.M.?), and again the map shows a stop in Williamsburg. I sit very still. Louisa has started to squawk in the bedroom. I get up from the couch and take a step toward her crying and then turn quickly back to the computer and lean down to the keyboard. My fingers fly across the keyboard, and the Croatian's Facebook page appears. I click on the "About" section and my entire body floods with relief as I see "Lives in: Upper East Side, New York." I am about to close the screen when I see the last picture she has posted. She is sitting cross-legged in a living room surrounded by boxes. The caption reads "Anyone wanna help me unpack?" And the tagged location is "Williamsburg, New York."

BEFORE

MARCO proposed on December 22. Two months later, on February 22, we were married at New York City Hall surrounded by both sets of parents; my sister and her husband, Tim; and Holly and Mike. Seb stood off to the side clutching the rings tightly in his hand. I spent the two months in between the proposal and our civil ceremony frantically completing Marco's green card application. We wanted to get our marriage certificate and complete the green card application in advance of our big reception in Maine so that we could go on a real honeymoon in a year's time. We had a free consultation with an immigration attorney soon after we returned to New York, but I was determined to complete the application myself and save the $1,500 for our honeymoon.

"Babe, are you sure we don't need an attorney? I don't want to mess around with something this important," Marco said as we walked out of the consultation.

"Sweets, I am positive I can do a better job than that attorney. This will be fun for me."

"OK, fiancée," Marco said, draping his arm around my shoulder. "If I end up being shipped back to Argentina, I expect you to come with me and learn to tango."

"At the very least, I'll totally write you a letter every day until I meet someone else," I said, and Marco swatted my butt as we walked into a coffee shop to Google "marriage-based green card application."

The very next day I spent four hours reading each form we would need to fill out, every question we would need to answer, the instructions that went along with every question, and the list of fees associated with the application. By the end of the four hours, I had a detailed cover letter written that laid out every single page to be included in our application. I let out a satisfied sigh, printed the cover letter, laced up my snow boots, and trudged through the icy sleet that covered the streets to the Rite Aid a block from our apartment. I bought a black binder, a photo album, and alphabetical dividers and trudged back home.

Over the next two months I spent hours working on the application. Calling and texting Marco throughout the day to ask "What are your parents' full names?," "Where is your passport?," "Why didn't you get an I-94 when you arrived in the States twelve years ago?" ("Well . . . the thing is, I kind of lost it when I moved a couple years ago." *Marco. Ugh.* OK, I'll figure it out, *gah!*") I made copies of our birth certificates, passports, bank statements, apartment lease, joint cell phone bill, and every other important document that existed; I printed out fifty pictures chronicling our relationship from the days at the burger restaurant up to the picture of us toasting our engagement with my parents and wrote a cute caption under each one ("First trip to Disney," "Vacation to Lake Luzerne," "Apple-picking with Sebastian"); I wrote affidavits that my parents and Holly signed, confirming their knowledge of our two-year relationship; I wrote addenda explaining each and every potential hiccup that could result in a delay or request for more information by the United States Citizenship and Immigration Services. ("Please note that Mr. Medina's I-94 form was lost; however, please find a copy of Mr. Medina's passport page showing valid entry into John F. Kennedy Airport on December 10, 1999.") By February 21, 2013, I had Marco's entire green card application neatly arranged in that black binder, organized exactly according to my cover letter, each document placed behind the corresponding alphabetical divider. The only dividers that contained empty space between them were A and B, and that afternoon, the afternoon before our civil ceremony, I opened the black binder and read aloud tab A one more time: Certificate of Marriage.

"Baby, look, look at that beautiful binder," I said, while packing up my overnight suitcase that I would be bringing to the hotel where I was staying that night. "I would like you to please admit that I was totally and completely correct about not needing a lawyer."

Marco opened the binder and flipped through the dividers. "This is amazing. You are so amazing. Should we celebrate your amazingness quickly before you leave?" he said, tugging at my belt loop as I zipped up my boots.

"My parents just texted that they're waiting for me at the hotel and then we're going out to dinner and I'm all dressed and I haven't put on makeup yet. . . ."

"And our boring married life begins." Marco kissed me softly. "You don't need makeup. Actually you look even more beautiful without it."

I smiled. "How quick are we talking? Five minutes?"

"Oh, I can get the job done in thirty seconds, max."

"How romantic." I laughed and pulled him close.

MARCO'S handsome salt-and-peppered father muttered, *"Muy rapido, no?"* at City Hall the next day after the jubilant female judge married us in less than five minutes. My dad replied in Spanish, "The ceremony and reception in Maine will be much more traditional, don't worry. Jenny and Marco wanted to get the green card application rolling so that they can go to France for their honeymoon next year." I wore a simple white vintage wrap dress I had found on Etsy a few weeks before with white satin heels, and Marco stood across from me wearing a gray suit with a black skinny tie and a nervous, adoring smile, and I thought to myself, *You lucky girl.*

We celebrated with our parents and my sister and Tim that night at Dos Caminos on Park Avenue South. Marco's parents were on a forty-eight-hour layover from visiting his sister in Denmark and were flying back to Argentina the next day, one of the major reasons we had picked February 22 to get married. Our parents had met for the first time that afternoon at City Hall and were now sitting across from one another at the long, rectangular table while Marco and I sat huddled next to each other across from Stella and Tim. I heard my mom and Marco's mom, Rosa, speaking loud, overpronounced words in English and Spanish back and forth, trying to decipher what the other meant and laughing. My dad and Marco's dad, Oscar, were carrying on a rapid, serious conversation in Spanish, Marco's dad waving his hands emphatically and my dad nodding and managing to keep up and insert a sentence now and then.

"Our rings look really good," I said, lining my left hand up with Marco's.

"I love our rings." Marco laced his fingers through mine. "And I love you."

"I love you so."

Marco excused himself from the table to use the restroom, and a moment later the waitress appeared and signaled to his empty drink, asking, "Would you like another?"

"Oh, that's my . . . husband's," I said, and then looked at my sister and screamed. I turned back to the smiling waitress and said, "Yes, my *husband* would love another one." My cheeks hurt so much that night that I had to suck my lips into a fish face on the sidewalk waiting for our cab to take us back to the Palace Hotel where we would spend our first night as a married couple (a present from my parents). I slipped into the cab beside Marco and rested my head on his shoulder.

"Wife, wife, wife," I heard from above.

"Husband, husband, husband," I said in return.

"My wife, my wife, my wife," he said.

AFTER

THE next day, Marco and I bring Louisa to meet Rosa and Oscar at a breakfast place around the corner from our apartment. When we walk inside, Rosa bolts up from her seat, half dancing, half running toward Louisa and me. Suddenly, tears are streaming down my face. "Please help me," I want to whisper to her as she takes me in her arms.

"*Mi amor?*" she asks, looking to Marco.

"Hormones, Ma," Marco explains in Spanish. "She's been hormonal and crying for no reason since Louisa was born. Everything's fine."

Rosa looks at me intently and then peers down at Louisa. "*Sí?*" she says uncertainly.

"*Sí.*" I nod and force my lips upward. "*Sí, sí.*" I want to tell her everything is not fine. I want to explain what has been going on the past few days, but it's clear Marco is not going to say anything and I don't have the vocabulary. Rosa and Oscar glance at each other worriedly over breakfast as I push home fries around on my plate and Marco robotically eats his omelet. I pray that they will notice something is off and ask Marco what's going on. I've felt close to Rosa and Oscar from the moment I met them three years ago, but we've always communicated in hand gestures and laughter. I can't explain what has happened in English, so how am I going to do it in a language I barely speak? *Please help me,* I want to say. *Help me get your son back.* Instead, Louisa stirs in the stroller, and Rosa jumps up from her seat.

"Preciosa," she cries as Louisa opens her eyes and stretches tiny fists into the air. For the next twenty minutes, Louisa is passed joyously between Rosa and Oscar.

When we get up to leave, Rosa hangs back to help me strap Louisa back into her stroller. I turn to her; I must find a way to tell her. Before I can get out any words, she wraps me in a hug. "Everything will be OK," Rosa says to me, rubbing my back. "Everything will be OK, *yo te prometo.*" I try to find the Spanish words to tell her that Marco has morphed into a stranger overnight, but my mind is blank. We walk out the door in silence.

———

THAT night, I'm awake nursing Louisa when Marco comes home. I finally tell him about all the research I've done and describe the symptoms of burnout and adrenal fatigue.

"Yes. Yes, that's exactly how I feel," he says.

"See? You're so overworked and overexhausted, babe. I knew it; I knew that's what's going on."

When I ask him about the Uber rides he sighs and says, "Babe. Like five of my employees live in Williamsburg. One of the bartenders and I share a cab all the time, and he lives right off Bedford Avenue. Please just stop."

The next time Louisa wakes up to nurse it is 5:00 A.M. and Marco snores beside me. I walk into the living room for a glass of water and see that Marco's phone is charging on the couch. After a year or so of being together, Marco and I started sharing all our passwords. We never sat down and decided to do it, but at some point Marco yelled to me from the bathroom to check if his boss had e-mailed him back. I remember tossing my phone to him as I walked out the door to bring Seb to school, asking, "Can you please respond to my mom's texts, babe? And try to sound like me!" Eventually we both knew the few passwords that the other used for everything.

My pulse quickens as I illuminate the screen and quickly type in his pass code. *I'll check his texts, that's all,* I tell myself, to reassure myself what I already know. I scroll through his text messages. Nothing. The last person he has texted is Nat, and I click their conversation. I scroll to the beginning of the thread and start reading. He is telling her about his numbness, and she is gently prodding him to cut back on work and that maybe this isn't the right time to stress me out with a mental breakdown. I smile. She has my back.

Nat: Dude, anyone working from 2pm-4am. every day is going to have serious problems. You need to take a break. Spend more time with Jen and the baby. Sleep all day. Cuddle. Seriously.

Marco: I guess. I don't know. All I feel is numb.

Nat: OK . . . but you still love Jen, right? I mean, if I
could choose a person to spend the rest of my life with, I
would definitely choose her hahaha.

Marco: I don't know. I'm afraid to lose the baby but
not her.

My blood turns to ice. Then fire. Then ice again. I stare at the
screen.

I have to get out of here.

I move on autopilot into Seb's bedroom, what is to eventually
become Seb and Louisa's room, and pull a suitcase out from under
the bed. My dresser has been moved into his room to make space
for Louisa's crib in our bedroom, and I open the drawers quietly,
stuffing clothes into my suitcase. There is a pile of clean laundry
on Seb's bed, and I grab handfuls of Louisa's baby clothes and
throw them on top of my clothes. I tiptoe back into our bedroom
and unplug my phone from the wall. I bring up jetblue.com and
find a one-way flight to Portland, Maine, for $250. It is too expen-
sive and I have never flown with Louisa and I am terrified.

I click purchase.

I have an hour to get to the airport. I lift Louisa from the
swing she is sleeping in and place her in the car seat in the living
room. She stirs and then falls back asleep. I walk back to the
bedroom.

"Marco?" My voice is shaking. "Marco? I'm going to Maine
with Louisa. I can't be here right now. I saw your conversation with

Nat, and I can't stay here with you." *This is your last chance*, I want to scream. *Please try, please choose us, time is running out.*

He opens his eyes slowly and sits up. "What the hell are you talking about, Jen?"

"You said 'I'm not afraid to lose her,'" I say, and start to cry again. "I have to go. I bought a flight to Maine. I can't be here right now. I can't take care of Louisa like this."

Marco is now out of bed, moving toward me swiftly, a wild look in his eyes. I walk backward down the hallway to the living room. He keeps coming. He is screaming. "You are the most selfish fucking person I have ever met in my entire life. What am I supposed to tell my parents? Did you think about that? They're here to see you and the baby. This is going to kill them, and it will be your fault."

I am all the way in the kitchen now, and I look around. I have nowhere else to go. He is still screaming, and his eyes are bloodshot. He picks up Louisa's car seat and walks quickly with her into Seb's bedroom.

"No," I say with a moan, and run after him.

"What the fuck is wrong with you? I am going to say goodbye to my daughter. Can you allow me that?"

I am seized with guilt as I imagine Marco's parents heartbroken. I text Sofia quickly the situation. "Please tell your parents I am so sorry, but I can't take care of Louisa here."

Her reply comes instantly: "Wait. Let me talk to them."

I shouldn't have told her until I had reached the airport. I am not going to be able to escape now.

"They're getting dressed. They're on their way over. Please don't leave until they get there."

Shit, shit, shit.

I look at the time. I now have fifty minutes to get to JFK. I hear the front door of the building clatter open and Spanish whispers drift up the stairs. I grab Louisa and my suitcase and meet them on the stairs.

"Lo siento," I say over and over. Rosa takes me in her arms. She is crying.

"Mi amor, mi amor, come with me," she says in Spanish.

"Calm, calm," Oscar says. His face is creased in worry, and he puts a hand on my shoulder. "Please go with Rosa to our apartment, and let me speak with Marco. Please."

I am trapped. I walk with Rosa to the Subaru parked right outside the building, click Louisa's car seat into place, and throw my suitcase into the trunk, and we drive the block to my parents' sublet. I lug Louisa up the stairs and into their apartment as she sleeps peacefully. Rosa immediately pulls out her cell phone and FaceTimes Sofia. When Sofia's face fills the screen, I tell her about the e-mail, the burnout, and the text conversation, and she listens silently. She speaks slowly in Spanish to her mother, translating everything I've said. I watch Rosa's eyes grow wider and wider, and then she covers her face with her hands and cries. Sofia says in Spanish, "Mama, she has to go home. If it were me in this situation, wouldn't you want me to be somewhere I felt safe? She doesn't feel safe with Marco right now. I don't know what's going on with him, but there's something wrong. It's not healthy for her and the baby to be around him right now." Rosa nods with tears streaming down her face and rocks back and forth, uttering, *"Dios míos, Dios míos."* We say good-bye to Sofia, and Rosa turns to me.

"Show me the girl," she says in Spanish. I bring up a picture and hand my phone to Rosa. *"No. Ay, no, no, no."* Rosa moans. My stomach twists. I don't have time to ask her what she thinks, and I'm not sure I want to know.

"Rosa, *lo siento,* I have to go," I say, and pick up the car seat. She hugs me and tells me that Marco must be sick and we will figure this out and everything will be OK. I nod. *"No sé, no sé,"* I say. *"No comprendo nada."* I get Louisa back into the car and pull away, glancing at the time. I have thirty minutes now before my flight boards. My phone lights up.

I pick up. "What?"

"My dad says I can't let you go." Marco's voice is dead calm now. "At least let me drive you guys to the airport. We can talk on the way there. Please."

I pause. My foot presses on the brake. "OK, I'm at the end of our street. I'll wait here."

By the time Marco gets in the car I know that I will not make my flight. He drives us halfway there, and then we turn around.

"Baby, when I had that conversation with Nat I was drunk and messed up in the head. Obviously I didn't mean that. I love you more than anything in the world. Please believe me; there is something very wrong with me. I think I have what you said . . . burnout? It's not that I don't love you; it's that I don't feel anything. You don't understand. I lost all my feelings. You are the most important thing in my life. Do you know how terrifying it is to look at the person I married, the person I chose to be with for the rest of my life, and feel nothing? I need your help."

My hands are clenched at my sides as we pull back onto our street. "I'm so confused," I say. "I don't feel well." How can I put into words that the person beside me is a stranger? That the person who felt like home now feels like a threat?

"We'll figure it out," Marco says. He parks and jumps out of the car, reaches into the backseat, and grabs the car seat. I sit, staring out the windshield.

"Jen. Come on," he says. He tries to hide his irritation, but I feel it, and the hair on the back of my neck stands up. I slowly unbuckle the seat belt and follow him back into our building as a feeling of dread spreads throughout my body.

BEFORE

A FEW months after we were married, Marco came home from a new bartending job and collapsed onto the couch.

"I can't do this anymore. I hate working for people who don't know what they're doing. I thought by now I would have my own place. I'm a thirty-four-year-old bartender."

"Well, then, let's start a business. Make a plan. Or at least start thinking about what you would need to do to get the ball rolling," I said, stroking his hair.

"Babe, if I owned my own place, I would make a killing. I've worked in so many different places, and I've seen what some owners do right and some do wrong. I know so much more than the asshole I'm working for now. It's killing me."

"I know you would be successful. I know you *will* be successful. I've always known that, Marco. You're such a hard worker. That's why I hitched myself to your wagon," I said with a smile.

"*We* will be successful, baby." He motioned for me to come closer and buried his head in my shoulder. "Thank you for believing in me. I won't let you down."

"I know you won't," I said, and pressed my nose into his nose for the thousandth time. "Is my nose less pointy now?"

"Your nose is perfect."

"No, it's too pointy, but good answer, as always," I said, and pressed play on the newest episode of *The Walking Dead*.

———

THE next afternoon, Marco called me on his way home from working brunch.

"Hi, babe, so I've been thinking about our conversation last night, and I've decided I'm going to make it happen. I'm meeting this old customer of mine, Steve, who always talked about opening up his own place as well. I'm going to see if he wants to partner up. He has a ton of experience in the restaurant business, and I think he'd be a good person to work with."

"Wow, that's exciting! That's great. Are you coming home after? I want to hear everything!"

At home, Marco told me that the meeting had gone better than he expected.

"Steve has been in talks with this guy Tommy, who owns Nosh and that new Italian restaurant down the street."

"Wait, do you mean the really formal fine-dining place that's always empty?" I asked, throwing frozen strawberries and almond milk in the blender.

"Yes, exactly. That's the whole thing, see. Tommy is desperate to sell his new place because he's already taking a huge loss on it. It's just not the right concept for the neighborhood. So he's been telling Steve, if he can get him a down payment of, like, twenty-five grand or so, the restaurant is his."

"Wait, he only wants twenty-five grand?" I didn't know much about buying a restaurant, but I knew restaurants in New York City sold for well over a hundred grand.

"Well, then Steve and I would apply for a small-business loan. Steve and his wife, Michelle, have already been thinking about it and since Michelle is Asian, she could get a minority small-business loan pretty easily. And we have a name: the Thirsty Owl," he said peering into the blender. "Can you make me one of those smoothies, too?"

"Sure. Wow, OK, wait, so this actually sounds really exciting. It kind of sounds like you chose the perfect moment to talk to Steve. I mean, babe, I could invest some of my savings account for the deposit," I said excitedly.

"I don't know, babe. Do you really think that's a good idea?"

"Well, I mean, if you guys have a sound business plan and concept, then yes, I do. I think that money is just sitting there, and I would rather invest it in my husband than do nothing with it."

I had a chunk of money saved up from working at the hedge fund and a couple of modeling jobs, so a few weeks later, I wrote Marco a check for twenty-five thousand dollars, and Marco, Steve, and I celebrated at Doyle's. "To our first restaurant, the Thirsty Owl," Steve said as we hit our glasses together. "Fuck yeah!" Marco said.

———

OPENING a restaurant proved to be a lot more stressful and difficult than any of us had imagined, and we ran into roadblock after roadblock during the next few months. Starting with the fact that getting a minority-based small-business loan was not going to be as easy as Steve and Michelle originally thought. They had gone full steam ahead renovating the restaurant after Tommy had handed over the keys, and now Steve and Marco were running out of money. The small-business loan was nowhere in sight, and I had written another check to pay for renovations and supplies. Steve, Michelle, and Marco were working in the space whenever they could, and they had decided that since the small-business loan was being secured by Michelle, the partnership would be split evenly between the three of them.

"This isn't going the way I expected at all," Marco said one night after painting the interior of the restaurant all day with Steve and Michelle. "We're out of money. The small-business loan people are fucking us. We should have closed on the loan weeks ago, and they keep stalling. And it seems Steve and Michelle are trying to push me out."

"What do you mean?" I asked nervously. "Why would they be trying to push you out?"

"They just never want me around. Michelle hates me because we have different ideas about how things should be done. It just seems like they both want to get rid of me."

"OK . . . ," I said slowly. "We just need to get everything out on the table. Let's sit down the four of us tomorrow and figure things out."

The next day, the four of us sat tensely around a wooden table in the empty restaurant, surrounded by ladders, tools, and dust. Marco started in on not feeling like they were a team anymore, and Steve and Michelle expressed that they didn't feel Marco was putting in as much effort as they were.

"We're here every fucking day, Marco," Michelle said. "You waltz in once in a while, help out for an hour, and then you're gone."

I squeezed Marco's hand under the table. "Don't engage," I communicated to him telepathically. Steve and I found ourselves in the position of acting as mediators between Marco and Michelle.

"Look," I said, "everyone is under a lot of stress. A huge factor is that we're running out of money and the small-business loan is a huge mess. Marco doesn't want to lose what he's already put in, and you guys have Tommy breathing down your necks wanting more money. Everyone is obviously under extreme pressure."

"She's right," Steve agreed. "Tommy has been saying lately that he's going to take back the keys to the restaurant and sue us for damages. We've basically torn apart his restaurant and haven't delivered the additional one-hundred-and-twenty-five K that we promised him would be here weeks ago. We're kind of screwed right now because of the small-business loan people."

"If I can scrounge up, let's say, another fifty K, would that appease Tommy for now?" I said, my mind working quickly.

"It would definitely get him off our backs for another few months. And by then the small-business loan will be here, and we can pay you back immediately and get Tommy the rest of his money *and* have some working capital," Steve said, and Michelle and Marco nodded.

"OK, let me talk to my parents and see what I can do," I said, my foot tapping fast under the table. As much as I hated to do it, I thought I might be able to approach my parents for a loan.

I talked to my parents that night, and my mom said, "I think it sounds like a good investment," and my dad said, "We will invest under one condition. You must be made an equal partner of the LLC. If you're putting up this much money, you need to be written into the LLC agreement and the four of you need to sign it before you hand over the money."

Two weeks later, the four of us sat around the same wooden table in the empty restaurant and signed the LLC agreement. Two weeks after that, the small-business loan closed and suddenly we owned a restaurant.

"Oh my God, you did it," I said after Marco got off the phone with Steve. "Not that I didn't have complete faith in you, but I was terrified for a while there that this was all going to fall through. Oh my God, babe! You did it!"

"We did it, baby. We own a restaurant. Holy shit."

"Holy shit."

AFTER

"I'LL get to the bottom of this," Oscar says calmly in Spanish. "If there is another woman, I will find out. Marco does not lie to me. Trust me, *mi amor*, I will get to the bottom of it."

I'm sitting cross-legged on the couch in my parents' sublet, where Rosa and Oscar are staying for the next two weeks. I understand enough Spanish to get the gist of what Rosa and Oscar are saying, but not enough to respond back correctly.

"No comprendo. No comprendo nada," I mumble. I've been repeating this phrase because I don't know what else to say. Rosa and Oscar have been asking me questions for the past couple of days, trying to understand the events leading up to my almost fleeing New York with Louisa. I tell them again about the e-mail and the change in Marco's personality the best that I can in Spanish, but none of it makes sense and we all feel it in the silence that follows my *"No comprendo nada."* I am clinging to Oscar's promise. He will

get to the bottom of it. If anyone can get through to Marco, it is Oscar, the man Marco has looked up to and respected all his life. I want to tell them I'm so scared. I want to tell them on January 20, the man I thought of as my protector, the man I thought of as my home, turned to me with dead eyes and said, "I'm looking at you and feel nothing." I almost want to reveal something, anything, that would make it make sense. That we've been secretly miserable for years. That we scream and fight every night and haven't been intimate in months. But I love my husband. I am terrified to be a new mother; I am full of hormones that caused me incredible unfocused anxiety the first few weeks home from the hospital, but I know that I love my husband in a way that I don't love anyone or anything else. My voice catches in my throat as I say one more time, *"No comprendo nada."*

Rosa and Oscar leave to go talk to Marco at our apartment. I have been spending my mornings with them in the bright two-bedroom sublet with a view of the Empire State Building. Marco has been waking up even later than usual, and I can't stand tiptoeing around our dark, stuffy apartment. Rosa and Oscar and I can't communicate much when we're together, but it feels oddly comforting to spend time with Marco's parents. The three of us are bonded by our determination to get the old Marco back.

This morning, I bundled Louisa up in her gray fleece snow-suit with bunny ears and hauled her down the creaky stairs of our grimy building and out into the fierce winter air. The sun cut into my eyes and the wind whipped my face, sharp as ice. I pushed her in the bright red stroller to the coffee shop a few blocks away, where I ordered a small latte. The cashier peered into the stroller and asked, "How old?" I told her she's five weeks today, and I heard the two women at the table nearby whisper, "My God, she looks fantastic." I almost turned around and told them that in the past seven days I've lost sixteen pounds, that I had plateaued a few weeks after giving birth but then discovered my husband is potentially having an affair and the pounds have melted off. Instead I plastered a smile on my face, pushed a blonde strand back under my hat, and rolled out the door toward Rosa and Oscar's.

Now I am waiting at their apartment with Louisa. They have been talking to Marco for more than an hour. I wait and bite my thumbnail. Finally, I hear keys jangling outside the door, and I stand up. They walk in the door, and Oscar says triumphantly, *"No hay otra mujer!"* I FaceTime Sofia to translate because I want to make sure I understand everything that took place. Sofia translates the conversation for me sentence by sentence. Oscar questioned Marco over and over again about the e-mail and the girl, and he is absolutely certain that Marco is telling the truth. There is no other woman. This girl is an acquaintance and employee, barely a friend, that he was trying to help. Oscar and Rosa are, however, extremely concerned about Marco's mental and physical state. Rosa's voice gets louder and louder, and her face twists up in worry as she explains that Marco isn't sleeping, isn't eating right, is working too many hours, and all of this has resulted in his loss of feelings and his change in personality. *"Enfermo,"* she tells Sofia and me, "very, very sick."

I let out a deep breath and suddenly realize I can't remember the last time I took a shower. Rosa watches Louisa while I stand under steaming-hot water and lather soap all over my body. I can hear Lulu's cries through the pounding water and bathroom walls, and I barely finish rinsing my hair before I twist the water off and towel myself dry.

"Gracias," I say, scooping Louisa from Rosa and bouncing her up and down.

"Tiene hambre," Rosa clucks. "Babies don't cry if they're happy. She must be hungry." I pretend I don't understand what she is saying because I don't know how to say in Spanish that I nursed her twenty minutes ago, that my nipples feel like they have been caught in a meat grinder, and that no matter what I do, Louisa cries for no reason other than that she is a colicky newborn.

"Gracias," I say instead. *"Yo voy hablar con Marco."* Rosa puts a hand on my shoulder and says in very slow Spanish that it's important right now to do small things for my husband: bring him a cup of coffee in the morning, give him a kiss before he leaves for work, rub his shoulders at night. *"Sí,"* I say, *"sí, sí, yo sé."* When I walk into our apartment, Marco is stepping out of the shower. I force a cheery "Hi, babe!" and ignore the dread in my stomach. "How was talking to your parents?"

"Well, my dad asked me if I'm having an affair a hundred times and I told him 'no' a hundred times. So it was really productive and helpful," he says sarcastically.

"They're worried," I say carefully. "They just want to make sure they know exactly what's going on so we can all start to figure out a solution." Marco walks toward Louisa and me in his towel. I lift my face for a kiss. He passes us without stopping, and I hear him yell from the bedroom, "No one seems to give a shit about what's actually wrong with me. All anyone cares about is that stupid e-mail. I'm going to drop dead, and you'll all still be worried about the e-mail."

"That's not true at all." My voice comes out weird and high and cheerful again.

After Marco leaves for work, I nurse Louisa and she falls asleep. I pace around the apartment, picking up tiny clothes and blankets, washing bottles with burning-hot water and sweeping the floors. I open the fridge and peer inside. When was the last time I ate something? I have had no appetite since January 20. I close the fridge and pour myself a glass of water from the filter, squeezing my boobs as I drink. I haven't leaked in six days, and in the back of my mind I wonder if I am still making enough milk. I remember back to the lactation course that Marco and I took in October. What did the instructor say? Something about how in third world countries malnourished women still produce enough milk to breastfeed exclusively for six months. "The human body is incredible," our instructor said, and I whispered to Marco, "That's crazy," and he whispered back, "What, baby? Sorry I'm texting with your dad about the Patriots," and I rolled my eyes and smiled. That means that my body can make milk even if I'm not eating, right? There is too much to worry about, and I push this thought from my mind and pour myself another glass of water.

Louisa wakes up with an abrupt scream that fills the entire apartment, and I run to her swing and lift her out. I strap the baby carrier that my mom got me as a baby shower gift around my body and stuff Louisa in as she flails and squawks. "*Shhhhh, shhhhh, shhhhh,*" I say, and power walk in circles around the apartment. The computer beckons to me, but I pass it quickly and avert my eyes. Louisa finally quiets down. I sit on the couch and tap my foot. I look at the computer. Fuck it. I open the computer and bring up the History tab again, my hands shaking. Nothing new. I log into Marco's e-mail. A few work e-mails and a link from his mom to an article about placing your faith in God. My breathing returns to normal. "Stop obsessing," I say out loud even though I am bringing up our Uber account at the same time. What the . . . There is a ride tonight from Marco's work to JFK. That makes no sense. Marco is at work. I sway my body from side to side as Louisa starts to wriggle against my chest. I pull up Facebook and log in as Marco. I search for the girl. There is a picture posted ten minutes ago. A plane ticket resting on expensively ripped jeans stares at me, and the caption reads, "Get ready Vegas. Here I come."

BEFORE

MARCO opened the door. "After you."

It was my twenty-eighth birthday. He kept the restaurant a surprise until the moment we walked up to the double glass doors.

"Oh my God, this place is beautiful," I said, stepping inside. The restaurant was somehow huge and cozy at once, with cavernous ceilings and brick walls.

The elegant brunette hostess greeted us. "Welcome to Mercer Kitchen. Do you have a reservation?"

"Yes, we do," Marco replied quickly, "under Marco Medina, nine P.M."

"Oh, yes, I see you right here," she said, scanning the computer. "Right this way."

Marco wore a crisp white collared shirt and nice dark jeans with a brown belt. He squeezed my hand as we descended a large stone staircase to the downstairs dining room.

"This place is incredible. I'm so excited," I said taking in the chic crowd.

"Yeah? I really hope you like it," Marco said nervously. "I read fifty Yelp reviews that were all five stars, so hopefully it'll be good."

The hostess led us to a cozy table against a wall and I slid into the banquet seat.

"You clean up nice," I said with a smile, spreading the white linen napkin onto my lap.

"You are so beautiful," he replied.

"Hey, I wasn't just fishing for a compliment." I laughed. "But thank you." I looked down at the menu and then back up. I started to say something and then stopped. "What?" I asked.

Marco looked into my eyes for a long moment. "I can't wait to spend the rest of my life with you."

"How do you do that?" I laughed.

"Do what?"

"Make the room stand absolutely still." As I scanned the entrées, my mind traveled to a Facebook status his sister had put up that morning. A simple question that had generated dozens of comments: *"What is more important in a partnership, being in love or being friends?"* Almost everyone had replied that friendship was ultimately more important than being in love. *"You need a strong foundation of friendship to make any long-term relationship work, because being in love will fade eventually,"* a cousin had written. But I disagreed. *"Both!"* I wrote. *"They're equally important. When you really don't like your partner, you need to be in love with them, and when you fall out of love with them, you need to like them."* It was something my mom had told me ages ago that my grandmother had told her on her wedding day. I had never found that before in any of my previous relationships. Someone had replied to my comment, *"May we all be so lucky."*

I lifted my head from the menu and watched Marco as he looked at the drink list. I had finally found both.

AFTER

I SNAP the computer shut. Rage starts in my toes and travels all the way into my forehead. I am going out of my mind with anxiety, I am barely making enough milk to feed our baby, and my husband is paying for a car service to take his (What is she? His girlfriend? His friend? His employee?) Croatian to JFK. I want to scream. I want to throw something. Instead I march into the bedroom and pull the still-packed suitcase out from under the bed. I reach for the car keys on the front table and drop them, my hands are shaking so badly. I bend forward carefully at the waist, pluck them up from the floor, and straighten up. Louisa stays quiet. I roll the suitcase down the stairs and onto the street. Hail pelts my face, and the street is slick with ice. I move forward slowly against the hail, protecting Louisa from the sharp snow with one hand and dragging the suitcase with the other. I throw the suitcase in the car. I trudge back to the apartment, up the stairs, and grab her stroller. I walk back to the car and shove the stroller on top of the suitcase. I am freezing cold, but sweat pours down my body. I un-strap Louisa from my chest and place her in the car seat and buckle her in. Her face crumples, and she starts to scream.

"It's OK, baby, it's OK. You're OK," I say, starting the car and blasting the heat. My heart is beating into my ears. I pull slowly onto the highway. The car is on empty. *Shit.* I pull off into the first gas station. The little store connected with the gas pumps is closed and the area is dark and deserted, but the pumps are on. Louisa screams full-force in the backseat as I roll to a stop. I climb out of the car. My feet crunch on icy snow that is starting to stick and accumulate. The wind whips my face as I make my way around the car to the gas door. There is a thick coat of ice sealing the gas door shut. *Shit again.* I walk back to the driver's door and wrench the car keys from the ignition. I take small steps to the back of the car and hack at the ice with the keys. This isn't going to work. I am going to have to turn back. Louisa is screaming so loudly now in-side the car that she is choking on her cries. My heart races, and I am seized with panic. Suddenly, a large piece of the ice falls away, and I renew my hacking with vigor, careful not to warp the car key. I chip away the rest of the ice and pry open the gas door with a gleeful whoop. I fill the car and pull back onto the highway.

"It's OK, baby, it's OK. Please sleep," I plead with my scream-ing baby in the rearview mirror. I drive slowly and steadily for two hours before I finally call my parents and tell them I am on my way home with Louisa.

"I'm sorry, I knew you wouldn't let me come in this weather if I called you right when I left. I couldn't stay there, Mom. I couldn't be there."

"OK, please keep us updated every hour," my mom says calmly. It is only the waver in her voice when she says "I love you" right before we hang up that betrays her fear.

I call Marco next.

"I saw the Uber ride to JFK. I don't know exactly what's going on, but something is not right, Marco. You need to figure out what your priorities are because I can't take care of Louisa like this."

"Are you out of your mind, Jen? That stupid girl needed to get to the airport so I got her an Uber. She paid me back in cash. What the hell is wrong with you? It's not safe to drive in this weather," he says, and I can hear the anger bubbling just beneath the surface. "Whatever, Jen, do what you have to do." He hangs up. My hands tighten around the steering wheel. Maybe I'm over-reacting. It's just a car ride. Thoughts fly around in my head until I will myself to focus on driving in a straight line.

Over the next three hours, I receive dozens of texts from Marco. They start out angry, and then by the end of the drive he is swearing that he will prove to me and everyone that he is sick, there is something wrong with him, but that he is still the man I married and that he is not having an affair. He will recover and be the husband and father that he knows he is.

By the time I arrive home I have been driving for eight hours, it is two in the morning, and I am exhausted. My parents are waiting up for us, and my dad grabs my suitcase and brings it up to my room. I tell them quickly about the Uber ride and Marco's texts during the drive home. My dad says, "You guys should get some sleep. Let's talk in the morning." I am so tired that I respond simply, "OK, that sounds good," and sink into bed with Louisa.

BEFORE

A FEW days after we officially signed the LLC agreement and closed on the small-business loan, I received an e-mail from the USCIS.

"Babe!" I screamed into the bedroom from the living room. "Our green card interview is August sixth! That's in three weeks. Oh my God, oh my God, oh my God."

"What? Seriously? Aah, I'm so nervous. I can't believe this is happening after so long."

"Do you know what this means? If we get approved on the spot, we can go to Argentina!" I checked daily the website Trackitt .com, which tracks green card applications and interviews all over the country. New York City was infamous for having the longest wait time in between submitting your application, which we had done six months prior, and getting your interview date. Some couples had been waiting a year for their interview. "I can't believe we already have our interview scheduled. Whoever put our application together must have done an incredibly thorough job," I said as Marco plodded into the living room and joined me on the couch.

"Whoever put our application together deserves to be taken on a date," Marco said, and lifted my feet into his lap.

"I totally agree. She also deserves a foot rub."

"Oh geez, here we go."

"I'm just kidding. Well, actually, no, could you rub my feet? They've been really tight lately. Thank you, my love. OK, *so*. Let's talk," I said, wiggling my feet on his lap.

"Talk about what, babe?"

"I mean, let's prepare for the interview. Like, prepare for the questions they're going to ask."

Marco scratched the stubble on his chin. "But, babe, we're a real couple. Don't only fake couples need to prepare their answers?"

"But think about how nonobservant I am! What if they ask me what color our bathroom is and I say purple?"

"Baby, I promise, we are going to pass with flying squirrels. They're looking for the Russian woman married to the super gay guy. We have nothing to worry about."

I smiled and said, "Flying colors. That's the expression."

"I think you can say either."

"OK. I love you so."

———

THREE weeks later, we sat in a large waiting room with a dozen other couples. I clutched the photo album tightly with both hands. When Marco pried one of my hands off the photo album and laced my fingers in his, I whispered, "Don't be overly affectionate. That's too obvious."

Marco laughed from deep in his belly, and everyone else looked up from nervous silence. "Baby," he whispered back, "we don't have to pretend. We just have to show them how we usually act, and we'll be fine."

"Do I have my nervous rash?" I asked, and pulled down the neck of my sleeveless blouse.

"Just a little," Marco said with a smile. "But you still look beautiful. Oh, oh, see, babe? We have nothing to worry about," he said, pointing to a man awkwardly holding hands with a woman at least twenty years older.

Before I could respond a stern woman yelled, "Medina?" and I jumped out of my seat. "That's us," I said sharply, and Marco stood up and kissed my forehead. "Babe. Calm down."

"I'm calm," I said as we walked toward the woman. "I'm totally calm."

Our interviewer started by asking Marco a series of very straightforward questions back to back. The last question was: "Have you ever been convicted of a crime?"

"No. Well, wait, I was fined once for smoking a cigarette on a subway platform," Marco said nervously. I shot him an "are you fucking kidding me?" look.

The woman laughed for the first time since we entered her office. "The US Government doesn't care about that, don't worry," she said, and proceeded with her questions. When she asked us who put together the impressive binder, I practically jumped out of my seat. "Me! That was me. Marco thinks I'm anal retentive, but I consider myself detail oriented."

"I wouldn't use the word 'anal,'" Marco said quickly. "I mean . . .

wait, sorry, I didn't mean to say that word during our interview, but she said it first." Marco pointed at me and blushed, and our interviewer laughed again and said, "Well you can thank your wife for her anal-ness now. . . . Oh goodness, that doesn't sound good." And then all three of us were giggling like schoolchildren.

"OK, I think I've heard everything I need. I'm going to recommend you guys for approval. You should have your conditional green card in a few weeks."

I smiled widely. "We were planning to surprise Marco's parents with a visit next month since he hasn't been home in twelve years. Do you think his card will arrive by then?" I asked innocently. On Trackitt.com I had learned that New York City offices were notorious for putting you in the "approved" pile and then taking another three months to actually send out the green card.

"Hmm," she said. "It shouldn't be a problem, but . . ." She turned to her computer and started clicking. "Let's see if I can get it approved right now for you."

I squeezed Marco's hand so hard that my fingers turned white. "Oh, that would be great," I said.

That afternoon we walked out of the Long Island City USCIS building with an official stamp in Marco's passport and an e-mail already in my in-box alerting us that his application had been approved. His card would be sent out shortly. Marco opened the big glass door and we descended the stairs in the hot sun, and when we reached the street we turned to each other and screamed.

"We're going to Argentina!" Marco yelled, and we high-fived.

Six months later, I watched my husband's face as our plane touched down in Buenos Aires, Argentina. His face remained absolutely still, but his eyes filled with tears, and I leaned over and whispered in his ear, "You're home, baby."

AFTER

THE next morning, I sit with my mom and Louisa around the kitchen table as my dad makes omelets.

"I really don't think he's having an affair. It's just not possible. Maybe because he's so overtired and overworked he's making really bad decisions and doesn't realize how inappropriate his behavior is. He says he barely even knows this girl and that she keeps asking him for favors and he feels rude saying no so he keeps helping her with stuff. Like the apartment and the ride to the airport. I don't know. . . ." My voice trails off. I'm not sure who I'm trying to convince, my parents or myself. There is a part of my brain that has already added up all the facts. But there is a raw, almost animalistic force within my body that is clinging to the possibility that Marco is telling the truth.

"If you really want to know the truth, why don't you check his phone records?" my dad says from across the kitchen. "I'm sure that will confirm exactly what Marco is saying. That they never talk. That they barely know each other." His voice is encouraging, but his eyes are hard.

"OK. I will." My stomach lurches and my hands shake, but I know what I will find. Marco is telling the truth. He has told me over and over and over. He is burned out. He is exhausted and overworked. But he is not having an affair. I open the computer and log into our Verizon account. I fumble around for a few minutes on the website and finally figure out how to pull up the call log for the past month. I select his number and hit enter. I start scanning the month of January. So far, so good. My eyes flick over the numbers, willing the digits I have memorized not to appear. I scroll through the first of January to the tenth. Nothing. Not a single phone call between Marco and the girl. I start to breathe more normally.

"Nothing so far," I say with a forced confidence. And then my stomach drops. January 11. 3:14 A.M. Outgoing call for seven minutes. That could be anything. It could be about closing the restaurant. January 12. Incoming call for twenty-two minutes. No, no, no. January 13. Outgoing call, thirty-seven minutes. I have stopped breathing. I feel a searing heat creep into my face. January 14 to the end of the month is littered with her number. Two minutes. Fifty-four minutes. Multiple times a day. There is an eleven-minute call last Sunday, his day off. We were together all day. My brain scans from the beginning of the day (brunch with Marco) to the end of the day (watching the first half of the Super Bowl with Marco and then picking up Seb for dinner). There must be something wrong with the cell phone company records. Some kind of glitch in the system. Wait. I look at the time stamp again. 9:05 P.M., outgoing call. My heart pounds as I remember Marco dropping off Louisa, Seb, and me at home. ("I'm going to pick up lunch meat for Seb's lunch tomorrow. We don't have anything in the house. When is the last time you went grocery shopping?") I push back my chair suddenly and stand up.

"Jen? Jen, are you OK?" my mom calls after me.

"Yes. I'm fine," I say as I walk rapidly into the living room, up the stairs, into my bedroom, and shut the door.

"You piece of shit," I scream into the phone as soon as Marco picks up. "How could you? How could you?" I can't get any more words out. I am sobbing now. Gasping and choking on air that doesn't seem to be entering my lungs.

"Jen, Jen, calm down. What are you talking about?" My husband's voice is thick with sleep and he sounds . . . irritated.

"I looked at our cell phone plan online. You call her every day. You called her when you went to the grocery store last Sunday? On your day off?" My voice is somewhere between furious and pleading with him to give me an answer that will somehow make this new information mean something other than what I know it means.

"OK. Jesus Christ. Yes. I like to talk to the person. OK? I haven't touched her, I haven't kissed her, I haven't fucked her. But I do like to talk to her." Now he is screaming at me. "Do you *want* me to fuck her? *Do you?*" I hang up the phone, shaking. I power off my phone as a call comes in from my husband. The part of my brain that knew all along now tells the rest of me, definitively: Marco has a girlfriend.

I run back downstairs and sit down at the computer again. I bring up the call log. I force myself to scroll back, back, back, and then I find the date I am looking for. The day Louisa was born. My eyes scan the numbers quickly and then I see it. 2:03 A.M., outgoing call for forty-three minutes.

Forty-three minutes.

I remember Marco kissing my forehead. "I'm going to get some fresh air, baby, and maybe grab a bite. Do you need anything?" I shook my head no and smiled groggily at him through my epidural. A few hours later, I was pushing out Louisa, my eyes wild, Marco pushing my knee toward my chest, and I looked at him and said, "I can't do this." The doctor said very calmly to the nurse, "The baby's heart rate is dropping. I need an oxygen mask and please get the vacuum ready." I looked around the room, thrashing my head from side to side as the nurse strapped on the oxygen mask until I heard Marco say, "Babe. Jen. Babe. Look at me." I met his eyes, and he held me there. "Look at me. You can do this. You got this, babe. You got this." And then one more push and I felt my body rip open, but I didn't care because Marco was right, and I gripped his hand and screamed and I heard him say, "She's here."

Forty-three minutes.

A few hours before Louisa was born.

I stand up and I feel the ground come toward me and the world is black.

BEFORE

SEB, Marco, and I arrived in Buenos Aires the night of March 9, 2014. The next day, Marco and I woke up to sunlight streaming through the windows of the immaculate guest room in Marco's parents' house. March 10, 2014. Marco's thirty-fifth birthday. I had been secretly corresponding with Marco's sister for months before our visit. Sofia and her parents were planning a surprise party for Marco the night of his thirty-fifth birthday. She flew in from Denmark with Domenico, now a bilingual three-year-old, a week before us, determined to witness her brother's first time home in twelve years.

"I will get everything ready for the party with my parents. Don't say a word to Marco. Erase this now!" Sofia had texted me a few weeks before our arrival. We hadn't spoken about it since, but I woke up that morning with flutters of excitement in my stomach. Marco didn't know a thing. I had made a point of asking him if there was a special restaurant he wanted to go to for his birthday dinner. He shook his head and said that this trip to Argentina was the best thirty-fifth birthday present he could have dreamed of, and he was looking forward to spending it quietly in his parent's home surrounded by his family.

"Happy birthday!" I squealed as soon as I detected movement beside me in bed. "Thirty-five. How does it feel?" I asked, propping myself up on my elbow.

"Tired. And old," Marco mumbled, and pulled the thin, white blanket over both our heads.

"Oh, stop," I said, snuggling into his armpit and peering through the tiny pinpricks in the blanket. "You're not *that* old. I mean, not compared to, like, a ninety-five-year-old."

"Oh, OK. You're going to get it now." The sleepy growl came from above my head as I tried to wriggle free from his fingers already digging into my sides.

"Babe, stop," I cried. "Babe, stop, I will scream and wake your parents."

"My parents are already awake," Marco said as the tickling grew more intense.

"I . . . will . . . scream," I gasped between laughter and yelps.

"You're lucky I'm so old," Marco said, pulling me back toward him from the middle of the bed where I'd managed to half escape to. "Much too old for you now."

"Oh, much. Much, much too old," I agreed.

———

THAT afternoon at lunch, I asked Marco again if he was sure about not going out for dinner and then shot a sly, meaningful glance at Sofia.

"Absolutely. I will be the happiest clam in the pond just being home," he said through bites of empanada.

As it grew closer to the start of the party, I began to worry. How would we get Marco out of the house unsuspecting? Did his family have a plan? Marco and I were in the living room chatting with Sofia. I thought about using the bathroom and finding Marco's parents to ask but then realized I didn't have the vocabulary. At 7:59 P.M. I decided I must have misunderstood the plan. Perhaps the party was canceled. Or I had gotten the night wrong. With a sinking feeling, I picked up a magazine from the glass coffee table and settled into the couch.

Seb trotted over to me and whispered, "What's going on?" I had let him in on the surprise party weeks ago, and he was just as excited as I was (and very proud that he hadn't slipped and mentioned it to his dad).

"I have no idea," I whispered back behind the magazine. "I think maybe I got the night wrong."

Suddenly, Oscar burst into the living room. *"Vamos, vamos,"* he cried, followed by a string of Spanish words.

I tried to keep my face blank and asked Marco casually, "What did your dad just say?"

Marco frowned. "He says we have to go to the grocery store to get food for tomorrow. My parents are so crazy. They go shopping at the weirdest times. I'll tell him we're not coming."

"Oh!" I said, and then backed off the ledge of excitement into neutral territory. "I think it would actually be cool to see an Argentinian grocery store."

We piled into two tiny cars. Marco, me, and Seb with his dad. Sofia, Dom, and Rosa in the other vehicle. A few minutes into the drive, Oscar's cell phone rang. He chirped into the phone and then hung up and fired rapid Spanish at Marco, to which Marco answered back at a similar speed and with obvious frustration.

"Umm . . . what's going on?" I asked.

"I told you we shouldn't have come." Marco groaned. "That was my mom. She wants us all to stop and say hi to an old friend on the way. This is going to take forever."

"I'm sure it'll be fine!" I said brightly, and squeezed Seb's hand in the backseat.

We pulled up to a large stone building. Seb and I exited the back of the car, and I sidled up next to Marco.

"I'm sure my parents wanted to stop by and say hi because this woman is super wealthy," he said with a laugh, and grabbed my hand. "They're trying to impress you."

"I'm impressed," I said, and winked at Seb.

Sofia, her parents, and Dom trotted ahead of us. We passed through two large wrought iron doors into a large lobby. Oscar had already talked to the security guard, and we continued down a long hallway. Up ahead of us, Oscar suddenly opened a door on the right side of the hallway and Sofia, Dom, and Rosa disappeared inside.

"Pa?" Marco started to say, and Oscar waved us toward him, *"Vamos, vamos."*

I practically pranced with glee through the door, into the pitch black that greeted us. All at once, the lights came on, illuminating a huge room set with a dozen or so large tables, fifty to sixty people lined the walls, and in the middle of the room a mariachi band sprang to life, spilling joyous, frantic music in the air.

Holy. Shit. I glanced at Marco. He stood stock still, momentarily paralyzed. He turned to me with wide eyes. "Did you know about this?" he yelled over the music. Now people were yelling and whistling. My eyes traveled to a banner that read "BIENVENIDOS MARCO, JEN Y SEBASTIAN." A fully stocked bar sat to the left of the band.

"I mean . . ." I started as waitstaff trickled into the room, passing out glasses of champagne. "Your sister said they were throwing you a surprise party but . . ." I looked around the room at the fifty smiling faces staring back at us, their bodies moving and hands clapping to the music of the mariachi band.

"Tonight," Marco yelled back to me, grinning from ear to ear and starting to embrace various relatives who were making their way over to us, "you learn to tango."

AFTER

MARCO and I spend the next few days on the phone screaming at each other. He sends dozens of texts a day that he is not having an affair, that if he wanted to cheat he would have done so a long time ago and with someone he actually found attractive, and that he has never even touched the "trashy kid," as he now calls her.

I can't eat. I can't sleep. I look at Louisa and all I see is my own fear reflected back at me. I am now on my own with a colicky newborn baby. I wanted a baby with Marco, but, before I met him, I had never longed to be a mother. The only thing that made motherhood less terrifying in the months leading up to Louisa's birth was "We're in this together." The thought of raising a child on my own never even crossed my mind. I am desperate to believe Marco so that I don't have to face this new reality, but how can I?

After I put Louisa to bed, I join the Single Moms forum in

my What to Expect pregnancy app on my phone. I quickly scroll through the discussions. "Taking my ex to court for child support," "Baby's first overnight with the new girlfriend," and "I can't do this—please help," flash across my screen. I click Leave Group with trembling fingers.

I pick up my phone and call Marco's best friend, Aaron. Marco and Aaron used to be neighbors; they lived in the same apartment building for a couple of years. Even though their friendship is relatively new, Aaron is Marco's closest, and really only, male friend. "Aaron, it's Jen," I say when he picks up. I have never called him before, and I rush to explain. "I know this is out of the blue, but things have been really fucked up with Marco lately—"

Aaron cuts me off. "He called me," he says with a small laugh. "Guys actually do talk when it's this important."

"He did?" I ask. "What did he say?"

"He told me everything. He told me about the e-mail and his physical problems, his loss of feelings, his numbness."

"Did he tell you about the phone calls?" I ask sharply.

"Yes, he did," Aaron says with a sigh. "Look I'm going to give you my opinion and then the two of you really need to work this out yourselves. It sounds to me like he stopped feeling like he could talk to you because you react pretty intensely to anything stressful, like about work and finances. He told me he got into a bad habit of talking to this girl about his anxiety about the Thirsty Owl and your finances because he didn't want to stress you out during your pregnancy but also because you tend to freak out about those kinds of things."

"But those are the kinds of things that married couples have to talk about," I start in.

"Look, I'm just telling you what he told me. In my opinion, at this point, it's much more important to figure out *why* Marco felt he couldn't talk to you, rather than focusing on what he's already done, if you want to save the marriage."

Maybe Aaron has a point. I do tend to get extremely stressed out, sometimes over everyday things. I am seized with panic for a moment as I imagine Marco feeling as though he couldn't talk to me about something so serious.

"Also," he says, and clears his throat, "I asked him man-to-man if he's cheated with this girl, and he told me no. I was like, 'Bro-code, man, did you hook up with this girl?' and he said they haven't even touched. Maybe it's breaking bro-code to tell you that, but I wanted you to know."

"That's good to hear," I say slowly. "Thank you, Aaron."

After I get off the phone, I pace around my parents' kitchen. If what Aaron said is true, that Marco has never touched the girl, then is it all in my head? Have I invented an elaborate story? Maybe Marco is truly just burned out. But the phone calls. I try to put my thoughts in an order that makes sense, but they race around in circles, crashing into one another. My phone lights up in my hand. I run into the living room and close the door.

I pick up and say, "I spoke to Aaron."

"OK, that's good, I'm glad," Marco says. His voice is warmer than it has been in weeks. "I want to be completely honest with you, Jen. I've kept a lot from you the past few months." My heart pounds. He is going to tell me he had sex with the girl. "I didn't want to stress you out during your pregnancy, and I ended up talking to someone else about things I should only have been discussing with you. I want to be completely honest. I started to get addicted to the attention I was getting from that person." I shut my eyes tightly. Here it comes. "I think I became involved in an emotional affair."

I open my eyes. "OK." I am shaking. "You called her while I was in labor." My voice cracks. "The morning Louisa was born."

"Huh?" Marco says. There is silence. "No, no, no, baby. I barely even knew her at that point. She started working as a server in November and then in December, right around when Louisa was born, she took over all the social media for the restaurant. Babe, do you remember right after Louisa was born, and I was on the phone in the room with someone about all the upcoming holiday parties?"

I think very hard through the tangles in my head. Yes. I remember my parents coming in to meet Louisa after we were settled in our recovery room. Marco took a work phone call and talked in the corner of the room for about ten minutes while my parents held Louisa for the first time.

"I remember you talking to someone in the room for ten minutes. But this phone call was for forty-three minutes and it was when you left to get food while I was sleeping."

"Right, but the call in the hospital room was a follow-up call from her. The previous call, I was going through her new job description as social media manager because I knew I wouldn't be able to in the upcoming days." His voice is steady and sincere. "After she became the social media manager, we started talking more and more, and I don't know how to explain it. I got addicted to the attention. But I never touched her, baby. I swear on Sebastian's and Louisa's lives." My heart rate slows, and I start to breathe normally.

"Marco, how on Earth did you let this happen? An emotional affair right when we're having our first baby together? Do you know how traumatic this has been? I don't even know how to process the past few weeks." I start to cry, but I feel relieved. We can work through this, maybe even get counseling. We can still be a family.

"I don't know, baby. I'm telling you this would have never, ever happened if I was in my right mind. I've been feeling so numb and . . . off. . . . It didn't even seem like I was doing anything wrong until now. Something really bad has happened to me. I haven't felt anything since the end of October. My insides are like a flat line."

We talk for a few more minutes about his physical condition and make plans to get him in for a full physical and blood work. He says his parents have left for Denmark to see his sister, and he has bought a plane ticket and booked a hotel in Portland. He'll be here in five days. "I'm going to fight for you," he says before we hang up. "I'm going to show you that all of this happened because I was very, very sick, and I'm going to bring back the man you married."

I walk around the living room trying to process everything. I hear the door creak open and my mom slips inside. She is carrying two glasses of rosé.

"I probably shouldn't be bringing you wine considering you've barely eaten anything in the past few days, but I figured you could use it," she says, handing me a glass.

"Thank you," I say. We sit side by side on the white couch, and I tell her about my conversation with Marco. My mom takes a sip of rosé and says, "So either he's a complete liar and he's having a full-fledged affair, *or* he's having some kind of emotional affair and also suffering from medical burnout."

I laugh. It sounds so ridiculous. "Yes, basically." I rub my temple and drain the last of my wine.

"Here's the reason I am actually inclined to believe that he hasn't physically cheated," my mom says, and my heart leaps in joy. "Is he really willing to risk everything for a twenty-two-year-old, selfie-obsessed girl? His green card, the restaurant, his marriage, his brand-new baby? He's been madly in love with you for five years. It doesn't make any sense."

"I know, Mom, I know."

"What he's already done is enough to end a marriage," my mom says, looking me in the eyes. "Normally, I would say it's time to walk away because an emotional affair, if that's what it is, is devastating, and he has broken your trust. But you guys just had a baby, so there is a large part of me that wants to believe this can be fixed." She looks into her glass, and when she looks back up her eyes are filled with tears. "I don't want you to lose the family and future you thought you would have. Not like this."

"I know," I say slowly. "I'm so confused."

My dad comes into the library. His face is unreadable. "What happened?"

I brief him. "He said he's finally being completely honest and that none of this would have happened if he was in his right mind," I finish, and look expectantly up at my father.

"Men do not have emotional affairs," my dad says simply.

"But . . ." I start and falter. "He said he was addicted to the attention."

"I am telling you what I know," my dad says. Each of his next words are crisp and hard, like a hammer pounding down a nail. "Men. Do. Not. Have. Emotional. Affairs."

"Robert," my mom interjects, "why the hell would Marco be sleeping with a girl he doesn't even find attractive when he has a beautiful wife and brand-new baby?"

"He's clever. He's telling you lies that sound like the truth."

I take a deep breath.

"Let me see this girl," my dad says.

I pull up the selfie on my phone and hold it up. My dad peers down at it.

"You need to make an appointment to get tested for STDs as soon as possible," he says matter-of-factly.

"Oh," I say. It is the only sound I can make. I hadn't even thought of that, and now my mind travels to Louisa. If their relationship started before I gave birth and I have an STD, she might, too. "Excuse me," I say quietly. I run to the bathroom and throw up into the toilet.

———

FIVE days later, my dad picks up Marco from the airport. He wants to talk to him on the way to the hotel. Before he leaves the house I hear him tell my mom, "I'll find out whether he's lying or not. I'll be able to tell," and then the door slams.

I wait on the couch, huddled up with a cup of tea.

"He'll know, Jen," my mom says confidently. "Dad has amazing radar when it comes to lying."

My dad walks in the door an hour later.

"How was it?" I ask cautiously.

"I couldn't get a read on him," he says. My heart sinks. "He was like a zombie. The only time he showed any emotion at all was when I dropped him off at the hotel and told him that whatever happens, it was a pleasure having him as a son-in-law."

"That's good, right?" I say hopefully. "It fits with him losing all his feelings. But the fact that you saying that stirred something in him I think is a good sign."

"I don't know, Jenny," my dad says, walking toward his bedroom. "I really don't know what to think."

I KNOW on Marco's hotel door an hour later. Louisa shrieks happily in her stroller. She is two months old today. I smile down at her nervously. Marco opens the door. We stand face-to-face for a moment. He is paler than I have ever seen him. His face breaks into the smile that I know, and I can't help but smile back.

"Hi," he says.

"Hi," I say.

I shuffle into the room, pushing Louisa ahead of me on the plush carpet. I catch my reflection in the mirror as I remove my winter coat and hat. I am thin. Too thin to have just had a baby. I look away in shame. I need to eat so that Louisa can eat. I settle into a wing chair beside the bed. Marco sits across from me in a computer chair by the desk. I look out the expansive window at the Old Port below. Marco and I have visited Maine so many times together that each section of this port city holds a different Marco memory. It used to be my city. Now it is our city.

"Marco," I say with a sigh. "Where do I even begin? I don't even know how to process these past couple of weeks. I don't know how we can ever get past this."

"OK," Marco says blankly. "I'll get a lawyer to do the divorce."

My heart stops. He says it like it is nothing. If anyone is going to be talking about divorce, shouldn't it be me? He came to Portland to tell me *this*? In a whirl, my mind travels back to the Square, meeting Seb, our engagement, Louisa's birth, and then zooms forward to the four of us celebrating Christmas next year, playing at the park in the summer, taking our first family trip to Buenos Aires. The past five years and the future I was so sure of evaporate in an instant. I want to yell, "That's not what I meant, please, Marco, please." But when I look into his eyes, they are dead. I gulp back, what is it, a scream? A sob? And reply as calmly as I can, "OK."

I stand up in a daze. "I should go."

I am almost out the door with Louisa when I hear, "Wait, Jen, please. I came here to make things right. I came here to get my family back." His voice is still monotone, but I want to throw myself into his arms. I want to shake him and scream, "Where is *my* Marco? I need him to come back *right now*." Instead I say very carefully, "We have a lot to talk about. We have a lot of work to do."

"I know. I don't know how we got here. I don't know how this happened." He pulls out his phone. "I'm going to give my two weeks' notice right now. This job almost killed me and broke our family. It's not worth it."

Three weeks ago I would have looked at him like he was crazy. Now I say, "I think that's a good idea," and try to keep the elation out of my voice.

He types on his phone for a few minutes. "Done," he says placing his phone on the desk. I walk over to him and wrap my arms around him.

"Jen." He puts both hands on my shoulders and then holds my

face. "My health is very, very bad. I'm not excusing myself, but there is something very, very wrong with me."

"I wish you had told me sooner. I wish you hadn't let it get to this point."

"I know. Me too."

"Marco, I have to ask." I take a deep breath. "Did you have sex with the girl? Or even kiss her? Did anything happen? I need to know the truth." My mind travels to the last selfie Viktorija had posted. Shot from above, she is wearing a lacy black corset. Her breasts spill out the top, and she is giving the middle finger. "Life's a bitch," the caption reads. It is the type of picture Marco would have shown me before and groaned, "Why does every trashy girl think she's Kim Kardashian?" But when I saw it this morning, my stomach dropped.

Marco laughs wearily. "Jen. I told you a hundred times. I don't find her attractive at all. Yes, I made a huge mistake by talking to her about things that I only should have been discussing with you, but it was never a physical thing. If I wanted to cheat, or if I did cheat, I wouldn't want to be in this marriage. I would walk away."

"Are you still attracted to me?" I ask.

Marco has always made me feel like a goddess, like the most beautiful woman in the world. I often caught him staring at me in the morning before I had any makeup on. "You're so beautiful," he would breathe. Now I am bracing myself for his answer.

"Of course I am," he says, and kisses me softly. The kiss grows deeper and we are on the bed, pulling each other's clothes off. I pray Louisa stays asleep in her stroller.

When we finish, he looks at me. "Why did you want to have sex?" he asks seriously. I can't read his tone.

"I don't know," I answer slowly. I pause and think about it. "I think I thought it would bring us closer together, and I haven't felt close to you for the past couple of weeks," I say honestly.

"Oh," he says, and quick as that, old Marco is gone. The stranger is back.

BEFORE

"OH my God," I said to Holly, Charlotte, and Stacy as they fastened the long, flowing veil to my chignon. "I look like you guys did," I said, remembering the awe I felt as I watched each of my closest friends get ready for their own weddings.

"You are simply stunning, my friend," Holly said, giving the veil one last tug to secure it firmly in place.

"And you can't see any bump at all," Stacy said from behind me in the mirror, eyeing my middle section.

"Really? Are you sure?" I asked, turning sideways.

"Positive," said Charlotte, straightening out the train of my dress.

Sixteen weeks ago I had gone out on a romantic dinner date with my husband and come home to find a pregnancy test that I had taken earlier that afternoon poking out of the trash.

"Babe . . . ," I called from the bathroom. "What the hell. What the hell."

"Did you say something?" Marco said. I emerged from the bathroom slowly to find Marco turning on *Game of Thrones* in the living room and setting two glasses of rosé on the table.

"What's wrong? Jen, are you OK?" Marco said, taking in my ashen face.

"Remember when I said earlier today, 'I better take a test just to make sure since I'm a few days late'?"

"Yes . . . it was negative. Right?" Marco said, eyeing the stick in my hand.

"Yes. It was. And now it's positive. What the hell?" I said again.

"Babe, I'm sure it got messed up from being in the trash. But maybe you should take another test. Just to make sure?"

"Um, yes, baby, I absolutely am going to take another test, but I don't have another one to take," I said. I whipped out my phone and Googled "pregnancy test turns positive hours later," as Marco started to put his shoes back on.

"I'll run to Rite Aid," Marco said, "but seriously I'm not worried. There is a one percent chance you're pregnant. And anyway, wouldn't that be kind of a good thing?"

"Oh, you know what, this website is saying that all pregnancy tests turn positive eventually. Something happens when the chemicals mix with the air. OK, phew. Well, you do keep saying you have baby fever, but I don't really want to find out I'm pregnant right after sharing a bottle of wine and taking shots," I said, laughing. Marco knew the owner of the French restaurant we had just come from, and at the end of our meal he had come over with two shots of absinthe.

I paced around the living room while Marco went to Rite Aid. "There is no way I'm pregnant," I said out loud. I sat down on the huge cream chair that matched the cream couch and then jumped up, remembering that this was the chair where, a month ago, Marco and I had thrown caution to the wind and gotten frisky without using protection. One time. "You can't get pregnant from one time," I said out loud again, and then thought immediately, *Of course you can.*

"OK, go go go!" Marco said, walking in the door, handing me a small Rite Aid bag.

I walked into the bathroom, my heart pounding, and came out three minutes later with tears streaming down my face.

"What are we going to do?" I said.

Marco stood up from the couch and walked toward me, his face breaking into a huge smile. "This is good news, baby. This is such good news." He wrapped his arms around me, and I fell into him and cried.

But he was right.

Eventually, my crying had turned into laughter and my worry had turned into excitement. We decided together that Marco would take a step back from the Thirsty Owl and start looking for a full-time, salaried job as a restaurant manager when we got back from our honeymoon. The team mentality had faded a few months after the restaurant's grand opening, and stress levels had risen. Tensions between the four of us were at an all-time high.

"I'm telling you, babe, they've been trying to push us out from the beginning. This is bullshit."

"How can they push us out when we invested so much money in the restaurant?" I said, pacing up and down the living room. "We can barely pay our fucking rent, and now I'm pregnant and I haven't even found a good doctor yet and—"

"Baby, stop. You have your rash." He stood in front of me and placed his hands on my shoulders. "You need to promise me that you'll let me handle this. You can't be this stressed out right now. When we get back from France, I will get another job that actually pays me and then I'll get your money back and we'll cut ties with those guys, OK?"

"OK. You're right. Let's try to get back whatever we can. I really hope I can get it all back. That money would be really useful now."

"I will take care of it. Don't worry about this anymore. At least not for another nine months, OK? Do you promise?"

"OK, I promise." From that moment on, I stopped waking up at 2:00 A.M. to worry about the restaurant and started focusing on being calm and happy for the baby. Marco sent me messages from his new job every night ("How are you TWO doing??") and—no matter how many times we assured each other that it might not be a girl—pictures of what our daughter might look like ("I can't wait for this!" captioned a picture of a man and tiny blonde-haired girl preparing dinner together; him chopping vegetables, her on a stepping stool watching in fascination.).

Standing in front of the mirror now, I looked at the bride across from me and touched my stomach. "Let's go see Daddy."

We said our vows in front of seventy-five of our friends and family with the endless Maine ocean as the backdrop. An old-fashioned trolley brought our guests to the oceanfront ceremony spot and then to my parents' house where a huge white tent was set up. We splurged on an oyster bar, top-shelf liquor, and a cheesy, fantastically talented band. When Marco and I arrived hand in hand at the reception after taking pictures at the ceremony location, the party was well under way. My sister gave the first toast. "Something I noticed right away is how much Jenny admires Marco, and I think that's so important in a relationship and in a marriage," she began. I nudged Marco with my elbow and whispered, *"Es verdad."*

"I remember the first time she really talked to me about Marco. It was near the beginning of their relationship, and she was really excited about him but I also noticed something else—I thought, *Wow, Jenny respects this guy,* and I remember thinking it because I had never heard her talk with such admiration or respect for a partner before. And then I met Marco and I understood why she felt the way she did." She spoke for a few minutes about respect and admiration being as important in a relationship as love. I squeezed Marco's hand. "That was a really great speech," he said.

"Well, duh, it was all about how awesome and admirable you are. No wonder you loved it," I said.

Up next was Seb, and before he even said a word there were whoops and whistles of encouragement as he very seriously straightened his bow tie and cleared his throat into the microphone. "Hello," he began. "Some of you may not know me, but, in a nutshell, I am Marco's son, Sebastian. I loved Jen as soon as I met her because, let's face it, you can't meet Jen and not love her. Her and my dad are a match made in heaven. If you believe in that sort of thing. I happen to be an atheist," the tiny black-haired boy chirped into the microphone, and the crowd roared in laughter. By the end of his speech, both Marco and I had tears streaming down our faces, and we were laughing hysterically. "Before my dad met Jen, he seemed like a puzzle with a piece missing, and Jen was that piece. I'm so happy that I get such an amazing stepmom and such wonderful stepgrandparents," he finished.

"He's amazing," I said to Marco.

"He's ridiculous," Marco said, and seized Seb in a hug. "That was great, buddy."

Right before dinner, the leader of the band tapped the microphone and said, "I'd now like to welcome the father of the bride to give his toast," and my body turned to spaghetti. My dad had been taking Spanish lessons for months, practicing the toast that he would give first in Spanish to Marco's family and then in English. I gave a silent prayer that he remembered his Spanish. I held my breath as my dad took the microphone.

"Before I give my toast, I'd like to say a few words to Marco's family, who have traveled here from Argentina and Denmark to be with us today." And then he began speaking in rapid, fluent Spanish and my mouth opened in shock.

"Damn, your dad speaks better Spanish than me!" Ian, Marco's goofy Puerto Rican groomsman, said.

My dad spoke for ten minutes in Spanish to Marco's family, and then switched to English for the rest of the guests. "I just spoke about Marco's character and how our family is so incredibly happy to welcome him and Sebastian into our family. I remember when I met Marco for the first time, I wasn't so sure."

Everyone laughed, and I clapped my hand over my mouth. "Oh my God, Dad."

"But then I got to know him, and I have truly found him to be one of the most kindhearted, hardworking, admirable men I could have possibly imagined for my daughter. She went through a lot of guys before Marco, and I was a little worried for a minute there that she might not ever settle down."

"Oh my God," I said, and buried my face into Marco. "I've dated, like, four men," I told the wedding party table.

"It has been a true privilege and honor to get to know Marco and Seb over the past couple years, and it is with great happiness that I welcome Marco into my family as my son-in-law." My dad finished his toast, and Marco's father rushed the stage to clap my dad on the back and thank him for his speech.

"That was epic," Ian yelled, and all seventy-five guests rose in a standing ovation.

We were about to sit down to dinner when we heard "Marco, Marco, *vien aquí*" over the speakers. Oscar had the microphone and was motioning Marco to join him onstage. "Oh, wow, this is going to be interesting," Marco said, standing up.

"Did your dad prepare a speech?" I asked.

"Nope," Marco said, "but don't worry, that's not gonna stop him."

"This is the best thing ever. I feel like I'm at the movies," Ian said as we watched Marco nervously take his place beside his father onstage. Oscar spoke for a full five minutes in beautiful, gorgeous Spanish, rolling his Rs and lifting his hands to tell his story. He handed the microphone to Marco and nodded.

"My dad said . . . um. This has been an amazing day, and it would be great if any of you guys wanna come to Argentina. You are welcome anytime."

Ian yelled over the laughs and claps, "Your dad is a freaking poet. That was like asking my cat to translate Shakespeare."

At the end of the night, Marco, Seb, and I all held hands and danced to the song "Happy" by Pharrell. I closed my eyes and tilted my head back, determined to soak in the last moments of the night. My mind rewound to the beginning of the day, and I pictured Marco standing across from me hours before, reciting the vows that it had taken him weeks to write, his voice trembling the tiniest bit.

Beautiful, today I take you to be my wife.

My promise to you is to be with you wherever life takes us,
    to unconditionally love you,
    to respect you, to protect you from harm—

I finished the vows in my head and opened my eyes to a blurry Seb and Marco.

"Do you think you should take a break?" Marco asked, eyeing my stomach.

"No," I yelled over the music, dizzy but happy. "I want to keep dancing."

AFTER

WE drive to my parents' house. Back at the hotel, Louisa woke up right as we were getting ready to leave. Marco picked her up out of the stroller and placed her on the bed between us. We spent an hour cooing at her. She laughed for the first time at the funny faces Marco made.

Please God, I think now, *please let Marco get better.* Glancing into the rearview mirror at the tuft of light brown hair peeking over the car seat, the thought fills my head, *Please let Marco love us again.*

We pull into the icy driveway of my parents' rambling white farmhouse. Candles glint in the windows, and snow hangs from the trees nestled around the house. Marco lifts Louisa out of her car seat and turns to me. "Well, this is gonna be awkward. I'm sure your parents hate me now."

"No, that's not true," I say. My voice comes out too high. "They're really worried about your health."

"Yeah, me too," he says, crunching along the driveway to the front door.

My mom greets us at the door and hugs Marco warmly. I give her a smile. *Thank you,* I say with my eyes.

A fire roars in the fireplace, and orange flames lick crackling wood. Marco and I sit side by side on the couch. Louisa sleeps in her car seat across the room. My mom offers coffee.

"No, thanks," Marco says in the monotone he has been using since January 20. "Coffee makes my migraines worse."

"You're getting migraines?" my mom says with interest, and settles into the white chair facing us. "I used to get them, too. The only thing that ended up working was acupuncture."

"Maybe you could try that," I say eagerly.

"Maybe," Marco says.

"So, are you invested in trying to make this work?" my mom asks, looking intently at Marco.

"Make what work." Marco's voice is a flat line. My face heats up, and I laugh nervously.

"The marriage . . . ," my mom says.

"Oh, yeah. Of course," Marco says quickly. He grabs my hand and rubs my palm with his fingers. The feel of his touch is foreign, and I almost shrink away.

"Of course," I murmur, and smile brightly.

———

A FEW days later, I take the first leg of the drive back to New York. We switch at a rest stop in Connecticut, and Marco drives the rest of the way, insisting that he feels well enough and that the pounding in his head decreased substantially in Maine.

"I wish we didn't have to go back to New York at all," Marco says, lacing his fingers through mine. "I feel sick just thinking about work, our apartment, the city. . . ."

Marco's health seemed to steadily improve over the three days he spent in Maine. Each morning I picked him up at the hotel, and we walked around the Old Port, pushing Louisa's stroller over the cobblestone streets and talking. We discussed the past few months and agreed that we failed on the communication front. Marco told me that work and the city were eating him alive and he kept it all inside because he didn't want to stress me out while I was pregnant. Each night he pleaded with me to come back to the hotel and stay overnight.

"I'm not ready," I said each time, "and where would Louisa sleep?"

The last night in Maine my parents babysat Louisa, and Marco and I had dinner at a beautiful restaurant in Portland. At the end of the meal, Marco took my hands in his across the table.

"Baby, let's move to Maine. This never would have happened if we had moved last year."

I thought back to last summer, when Marco had pleaded with me to move to Maine.

"I'm so tired of New York. Let's buy a small house in Portland and start new," he'd said.

"But what about the restaurant? I know we're trying to cut ties, but I don't think we should up and leave before we get our investment back. And my career? I need to be in New York. Let's give it another couple years. I want to move from a good mental place, not because we're struggling."

"I guess. Yeah, you're right. I do want to open my own place in New York. No partners. Just us two," he said thoughtfully. "OK, another couple years. Let's go out with a bang." He kissed my hand. "You're so amazingly wise."

I guess I hadn't been so wise after all. A year later, sitting across from him in the dimly lit restaurant, I squeezed his hand and said, "Yes. Yes, let's move. I can't stand New York anymore either."

"Really? Are you serious?" he asked.

I nodded, and he said, "OK, I'll finish out my two weeks at the restaurant and then we'll sublet our place." He took a sip of water. When he set down his glass, his eyes were wet. "I can't believe I let it get to this point. I held so much inside that I almost broke our family," he said as a single tear rolled down his cheek.

That night, I texted him good night from under the covers of my childhood bed.

"Good night," he responded right away. "I love you both so much. This is cheesy, but this is how I feel right now." A link came in, and I clicked it. Aaron Neville's voice filled the air as a live performance video of "Don't Know Much" filled my iPhone screen. I smiled and texted back, "I love you, too. But it's time to let actions speak louder than words."

Sitting in the passenger seat of the car now, I drum my fingers against his hand and look out the window. "I don't want you to have *any* kind of relationship with that girl during your last two weeks, Marco," I say seriously. The New York City skyline looms ahead us.

"Well, I work with her, so I'm going to have to see her, but I promise you, as soon as I leave that place, I will never, ever see her or speak to her again." He sighs. "I've told you a hundred times, there was never any physical attraction. She wears so much makeup that she looks like a clown half the time. You know I'm afraid of clowns."

This shouldn't make me happy. I've never been catty. But I allow myself a little snort.

———

THE first night back in New York does not go well. Marco had put a picture of my sunglasses on his Instagram account while we were in Maine and tagged me in the photo. Normally, I wouldn't have even noticed, or I would have teased him about tagging me in all his pictures, but when I got the alert on my phone a couple of days ago, I was ecstatic. Marco hadn't put up any pictures of me or Louisa since January 20. I was in a good place when he left for work, but when I noticed that the tag was removed from the photo, my whole body clenched.

"Why did you remove that tag?" I text him immediately.

"What are you talking about?" he replies ten minutes later.

"The sunglasses picture. What the fuck, Marco?" It is small and stupid and shallow, but I am enraged.

"Wow. I didn't untag it. And you sound insane." I start to write back more expletives and stop. Maybe I do sound insane. Maybe his phone untagged it somehow. Maybe he never tagged me in the first place. I try to remember back to the exact moment I received the alert. I can't think. Everything is blurry. I decide to drop it.

The next few nights are worse. Every day we spend a few nice hours together before he has to leave for work. Every night, as soon as the sun sets, I start to feel nervous, jittery, like a hyena circling prey. "Are you sure she's not there tonight?" I text before I can stop myself.

"Babe. Stop," comes his reply.

We just have to make it ten more days, I think to myself. I have rented a storage unit for our belongings. We leave for Maine at the end of the month. My parents have moved back into their sublet. They will drive back to Maine the last day of February and we will follow them in the Subaru. We decided that we will spend a couple of months on Peaks Island, in my parents' summer cottage, which is empty every winter. Just the three of us. We will cook together, cuddle with Louisa, sip coffee by the fire. Ten more days.

———

BUT I cannot wait ten more days. A sickness has been spreading through my body. I'm infected, consumed. I have to know for sure. I know what I have to do.

I pace around the apartment all night and at around 2:00 A.M., I start getting ready. I gently lift Louisa from her swing and strap her into the car seat. She stirs for a moment and then settles back into a deep sleep, her mouth slightly open, her eyelids twitching. "I'm so sorry, baby," I whisper. "This will be over soon." I put my coat on and then lace up my boots. I feel a cold sweat trickling down my sides, but I keep moving. I lug Louisa down the stairs, out the front door, and march to the car. There is a cold, hard ball in my stomach, and my bowels feel loose. I click Louisa into the backseat; I climb into the driver's seat, turn on the ignition, and yank the car into drive. I wait for the car to warm up and then blast heat into the icy, still air. "Please stay asleep," I whisper into the rearview mirror. The streets, a few hours earlier teeming with people, are empty, and I make good time. Sallow yellow light illuminates patches of deserted sidewalk. I stop at a red light and stare straight ahead. "Give me a sign, and I'll turn around," I whisper. The pit in my stomach grows as I near my destination.

I circle, finding a good spot to park. I dim the headlights and wait. The car grows chilly. I focus on the blood pumping through my body and into my ears. I rub my hands together and check on Louisa. She is toasty warm beneath a soft blanket. I turn back from watching her peaceful breathing and see two people exiting the restaurant. I am close enough to make out his crisp dark-blue suit and her messy, long blonde hair. My heart starts to thud. He locks the restaurant door, and they stand there for a moment chatting. He puts his arm around her shoulders and then takes his arm away quickly. She folds her arms across her chest. They start to walk down the street. I wait for them to disappear around the corner, and then I start the Subaru. My leg is shaking so badly that I hit the gas hard and jolt forward. I crunch along the cobblestone street, hunched forward, gripping the steering wheel. When I roll to the end of the street, I look right. My eyes strain, and I see the dark figures two street blocks away. I put on my blinker even though I am the only car on the street and start to turn and then see a ONE WAY sign telling me to turn left. Fuck. I am going to lose them. I jam the blinker stick in the opposite direction and hit the gas.

I turn left and go as fast as I can on the small, twisty downtown streets, until I reach a street that I can turn right onto. I turn right and then turn right again and drive straight for a few blocks, praying that I am traveling parallel to the couple. I turn right again and come up to the one-way street. I turn my head side to side, wildly, trying to spot them. The street is deserted. There is no one. *Fuck.*

I pull out my phone and quickly bring up Find My iPhone. Marco and I know each other's passwords in cases of emergency, and I type in his login information quickly. *Come on. Come on. Load.* A map appears and a dot shows me Marco's phone. I zoom in. I look at the dot, and then I glance at the street signs surrounding me. He is here. He is right here. I turn my head again wildly from side to side, straining my eyes. No one. My breathing escapes my body in haggard spurts, and I squint at the buildings, trying to find a bar, a lit-up window, anything. There is nothing. The buildings are dark. I don't understand. I take a deep breath and think. Something is wrong. I push a button on my phone and press it up to my ear.

"Hello?" Marco's voice rises above background noise of loud music and people talking.

"I know where you are right now," I say, my voice shaking.

"Jesus Christ, babe. You need to cut this out, seriously." He sounds far away.

"I saw you," I say, steadying my voice.

"What? What are you talking about?" I imagine him pressing his finger into his ear, straining to hear me over the loud music.

"I saw you put your arm around her," I say clearly. "I'm here."

"What do you mean you're here?" His voice is calm.

"I sat outside your work. And now I'm at West Broadway and Chambers Street. Your phone says you're here, but I don't see you."

"Stay where you are," he says quickly. "I'm at a bar up the street. I'm just dropping off the restaurant keys with the opening bartender. I'm coming out. Stay where you are."

I feel strangely calm. This is it. This is the moment I will finally know the truth.

Marco climbs into the passenger seat and quickly turns to look at Louisa.

"She's asleep," I say. It comes out normally, as if we're a family about to head to the park for a picnic. "I know now, Marco," I say just as smoothly. "I saw you put your arm around her." I put the car into drive and pull out into the street. A feeling of deep calm floods my body. "I finally know," I say serenely.

"Babe. Did you also see that I took my arm away fast and we didn't touch at all after that? Sweetie, she was cold and she shivered so I put my arm around her shoulders without thinking and then took it off really quickly. Just like I would do for your mom . . . or Nat. I didn't even think about it." His voice is steady. "I'm not having an affair. You want it to be true, but it's not."

Oh no. No. My stomach twists and the calm seeps out of me. Tears trickle into the collar of my coat. Please. Please just tell me. "I can't do this," I say. "I can't do this."

"Pull over, baby. Let's switch. You're shaking." We switch places, and Marco steers the car toward the bridge linking Manhattan with Queens. I lean my head into my hands and say again, "I can't do this."

"I know. The fact that you were spying on me, that you brought Louisa out in the middle of the night . . ." Marco's voice is soft and sad. He pulls one of my hands from my face and holds my hand tightly. "I never touched her, Jen. Never."

I stare straight ahead through the windshield. The lights lining the sides of the bridge blur my vision into a twinkling mass. I am going slowly insane.

BEFORE

"PLEASE tell me you're close." I sucked in my breath and closed my eyes as a wave of grinding pain wrapped itself around my midsection. "I really think this is it."

"I'm leaving work right now, baby." Marco's voice traveled quickly through the phone.

"Please hurry."

At the hospital we filled out paperwork, and I changed into a thin blue gown.

"They're going to send you home," I heard the receptionist tell Marco as he dropped off the clipboard. "I can see it on her face; she's not ready yet. Trust me, if that baby was coming any time soon, her face would not look like that."

The doctor said the same thing as she pulled on her gloves. "I'm going to check your dilation and we'll do a swab to see if there's any amniotic fluid, but my guess is we'll send you home for the night. Take a nice bath, relax, and see how you feel tomorrow. Sometimes Braxton-Hicks can feel like the real deal and then suddenly they just go away."

"Ugh, I really thought this was it," I said with a small laugh. "Maybe it's the full moon."

"See," the doctor said warmly, her head blocked by my huge belly, "if you were really in labor you would not be able to laugh. Trust me."

She left, and I tried to relax. A wave of pain rolled through my body. A few minutes later the doctor came back in with a young resident. "So, actually—oh OK, that's a face I recognize."

"She started having really bad contractions as soon as you left," Marco said.

"Well, what I was going to say is that the test came back positive for amniotic fluid. Your water hasn't broken completely but it's leaking, so I was going to admit you anyway. You were right. This baby is coming soon."

Within an hour the contractions were so intense that I pressed the call button for the nurse. "I need the epidural," I moaned through gritted teeth.

"The doctor would really like you to wait till you're at least a six, honey. It's only been an hour so you've got a while to go," she said calmly in a rhythmic Jamaican accent. "But I'll check you again, OK?" she added as I let out a long, guttural growl.

"Oh," she said slowly from between my legs. "OK, you're ready for the epidural. You're between a six and a seven!" She let out a loud laugh.

"Thank God," I groaned as a contraction wrapped itself around my insides like a bicycle chain and squeezed.

———

THE epidural kicked in instantly. "Baby, this is amazing. I'm floating." I smiled at Marco. "Ha-ha, that's awesome, babe. I'm going to get some food and some fresh air. Do you want anything?"

"No thank you," I said, my eyes closing. "I'm perfect."

———

WHEN I woke up, the doctor was in the room. "Good morning! So. The epidural slowed things down quite a bit, but you should be ready to push now. Let me just check you."

"Babe?" I searched for Marco groggily. "Are my parents here?"

"They're here, baby. They're in the waiting room." He took my hand. "How do you feel?"

"Good. The epidural is amazing."

"You said that, babe." Marco laughed.

"OK," the doctor said, motioning to the resident to stand beside her. "Let's do this."

I squeezed Marco's hand. "Are you ready?"

"Nope. Are you?"

"Yes. I think so." I gripped his hand tighter.

"OK, Mom." The doctor settled into a stool at the foot of the hospital bed. "Whenever you feel the next contraction coming, I want you to ride the wave and push with it, OK? It will feel like you're having a bowel movement. That's where I want you to push from, OK? And, Dad, take Mom's leg right there, and push it as hard as you can toward her chest when I say so, yep, just like that, you got it." She glanced at the monitor. "Are you ready? I see a contraction coming."

"Wait, wait," I cried during my first push, "I need to use the bathroom."

"Nope, that's the baby, honey. You're doing fine, keep pushing."

"Marco, am I shitting myself right now?" I asked.

"I don't think so, babe, you're doing great," he said as the doctor called from below, "OK, this baby is coming fast and furious. I need you to give me a really big push, OK?"

"Wait, I can't do this," I said, searching for Marco's eyes. "I can't do this," I said again as I felt an enormous pressure trying to rip through my pelvis. The monitor made a beeping noise beside me. "We need this baby out on the next push," I heard the doctor tell the resident.

"I can't breathe, I can't breathe." I clawed at the oxygen mask that had just been placed over my nose and mouth. Marco lifted the mask from my face and held my gaze. "One more push, baby. You got this. One more push and she's here."

FIFTEEN minutes after my first push, a long, skinny, red-faced, wrinkled baby was placed on my chest. "She has my eyebrows, babe." I stared at the huge eyes below my chin.

"She has your everything, baby." Marco laughed and brushed damp hair off my forehead. "Thank God."

AFTER

THE next morning, while Marco is sleeping, I shove fleece booties on Louisa's feet and hoist her onto my hip. We walk the three blocks to my parents' apartment under the glaring winter sun. I am still deciding whether to tell my parents about last night as I climb the last set of stairs to their apartment.

"Dad had a good idea," my mom says apprehensively as I walk through the door. "He thinks you should call the hotel in Portland and see if Marco made any calls from the hotel phone."

Ever since I found the phone calls in our Verizon account, there has not been a single call or text between Marco and the Croatian. I am satisfied that the emotional affair has ended. In the dark depths of my mind, I wonder how they are still communicating. Somewhere else, in the same depths, I am still clawing for the truth. If I can just know for sure, I will know what to do.

"OK," I say. I am no longer hungry for the eggs sizzling on

the cooktop. I walk numbly into the second bedroom and close the door.

"Hi, I stayed at your hotel with my husband a few days ago. We completely forgot to take the bill with us and we need an itemized receipt for tax purposes," I say brightly to the woman on the other end of the line. I give her my husband's name and my e-mail address. She says no problem, that John from accounting will e-mail that right over to me. My hands are shaking as I re-fresh my e-mail over and over. When the e-mail appears, my hands are shaking so badly that I almost drop my phone. I hun-grily click the PDF attachment. My vision is blurry, and adrena-line courses through my veins. One phone call. Fifteen minutes long. The first night of his stay. The numbers that I know by heart glare back at me.

"Anything?" my dad asks when I walk back into the living room. Both my parents look at me expectantly.

"Someone's going to e-mail me the bill," I say. I am not ready to divulge this last bit of information. I am not ready because it will be the same thing as saying, "My marriage is officially over." So instead I say, "I'd like to go pack a small bag while Marco is still sleeping. I think I'm going to stay over here tonight with Lulu." I know my parents will not object to this.

"That's a really good idea," my dad says, and my mom nods.

I lace up my boots quickly. I take the steps down to the lobby of the building three at a time and take a left out of the front door toward my apartment. I walk the three blocks to our building as quickly as I can over the ice and snow. My insides are jumbled. There is one wave of rage and one wave of sorrow mounting inside me. They collide together and then crash down, the white foam bubbling into one giant mass. When I reach our building, I slow down. I climb up the stairs slowly. These are the last moments before the end of my marriage, before I am officially on my own with a newborn baby. There is nothing that Marco can say to make this transgression OK. To explain it away. And suddenly it dawns on me. It never mattered if there was physical cheating. My marriage was over when Marco laughed his sweet, incredulous laugh on the other end of the phone on January 20.

I turn the key slowly and push open the door. The living room is cluttered with blankets and baby clothes. I take a deep breath and walk down the hallway into our bedroom. I watch Marco sleeping for a few seconds. Even in his sleep now, he looks so different to me. A stranger. The thick, dark, unruly hair that I used to stick my fingers in to scratch the scalp below is now neatly slicked back. It even looks darker. Or is this just my mind playing tricks on me?

"Marco," I say. His eyes twitch. "Marco, wake up," I say loudly. He groans and rolls away from me.

"What?" he mumbles to the wall.

"You called her from the hotel. You called her from Maine." My voice is strong and steady and emotionless.

"What?" He groans again. "Jen."

"Yes, Marco?" I say, daring him to explain.

He rolls toward me. His eyes are open. He sits up in bed and rubs his eyes. "I only called her the first night," he says. "I told you, I like the attention." His voice is weary. He's not even putting up a fight.

"You called her from Maine," I repeat. I sink to the floor. I hug my knees and tell him that I want a divorce. I get up off the ground slowly and start to pack a bag. While I am robotically shoving underwear and sweaters into my bag, Marco says from the bed, "I just want you to know something. For your own peace of mind. I never touched her. I know you don't believe me, but I want you to know that, even though I know our marriage is over. I never touched her, Jen. I respect you too much."

Tears fall from my eyes. I'm not sure if I am crying because I believe him or because I don't believe him.

"I just need to do one thing before I leave," I say. I walk over to the bed, to this stranger in our bed and push my nose into his one last time. He doesn't say "Your nose is perfect" this time. He doesn't say anything at all, and so I walk back down the hallway, down the stairs, out of our building, and onto the street.

THAT night I sit with my mom on the couch in their living room, nursing Louisa, and tell her about the phone call from Maine. I tell her that my marriage is over. She shakes her head and turns toward the window. I think she is going to rail against Marco, but when she turns her head back, her face is blotchy and she is crying. "It just doesn't make any sense," she says through a sob. I have a flash of murderous rage. I understand in that moment a tenth of what my dad has been feeling these past few weeks as I've cried out more tears than it seems possible a human body could hold. Why he is silent except for the grinding of his teeth.

I climb into bed with Louisa. She falls asleep on my chest, and tonight I keep her there instead of carefully transferring her to the swing. I wake up to her squirming and reach for my phone. I see that it is 5:00 A.M. and that I have a dozen text messages from Marco.

Placing Louisa on my breast, I scroll through the messages. The last one is from a few minutes ago, and it reads, "Can this really be the end? All I ever had was good intentions. There's no point in me being alive anymore. Everyone would be better off if I was gone."

"Marco?" I write. "Are you still awake? Where are you?" My heart pounds and everything is wiped from my mind except for, *Please be OK.*

"Still at work," comes his reply. "I don't want to go home."

"You should go home and sleep," I write, unable to stop myself from giving this wifely suggestion. I wait for his response. Two minutes go by. Then five. Finally, I see the dot-dot-dots, and I know he is not alone. He was waiting for the right moment to text, when she wouldn't notice. All of my worry and fear is replaced by rage. Louisa has fallen asleep nursing, and this time I gently drop her into the swing. I call the restaurant phone. It rings once, twice, three times and then Marco's slurred voice fills my ear.

"Hello?"

"Is she there with you?" I will be made a fool of no longer.

"No. Jesus Christ."

"Say it, Marco. Say she's not there."

There is a long pause, and then his voice comes out muffled and slurred, "She's not here."

"I love you, Marco." Fuck you, Marco.

"Mhmm," he mumbles.

"I love you," I say again sharply. We have almost never ended a conversation without saying those three words. I am going to call his bluff once and for all. There is another long pause and then, "I love you, too." I hang up. I am seething. Murderous thoughts race through my mind for a few minutes. I check the Croatian's Facebook and Instagram profiles and see that she has already unfriended and unfollowed Marco. I take screenshots of the last dozen messages Marco has sent me and fire them off to her. I am acting on pure seething anger now. I want him to be left with nothing. I click my phone off and lay my head down on the pillow. It feels like I have been sleeping for five minutes when my eyes open to sun spilling through the curtains and Louisa's squawks.

The next few hours I feel sick to my stomach. What if I'm wrong? Maybe she wasn't there. Maybe they are just close friends. Around noon, I am playing with Louisa on the bed. My parents have gone out to get lattes from the fancy, boutique coffee shop around the corner. I hear a buzz and squint at my phone on the end of the bed. I see "Viktorija" at the top of a text message and my heart starts to pound. I grab my phone and swipe open the message. Her response flashes onto my screen: "What a pussy lol. I am so done with him."

My pulse quickens as I read her next messages. "I have a limit and he crossed that limit last night. He is a pathetic excuse for a man. He wanted the best of both worlds, but he fucked with the wrong blondes lol."

"Will you please tell me once and for all if the two of you had a physical affair?" I write.

"You know everything now. I am so glad I will never have to see that piece of shit again after his last day. Looks like history is repeating itself."

History is repeating itself? I stare at the last sentence for a moment before it sinks in. Tania. The part of the story of how Marco and I met that I don't tell anyone, not even myself. The night he showed up at my door with his small black duffel bag and dark circles under his eyes: "Tania saw texts between us and went insane. She hit me and threw my phone. Can I please stay with you for a few nights until I can find my own place?"

He explained that they were still living together and, even though he had broken up with her dozens of times, Tania just wouldn't let him go. I push the memory from my mind and look back to my text messages as two new messages come in.

"Nat was the smart one. She left him."

How does she know that? And then I realize. He told her the same stories that he told me five years ago.

We text for a few more minutes. I tell her that it's very hard to believe that this was strictly an emotional affair.

"You really need to ask your husband these questions, not me. But I will tell you, we did not have sex. I'm going to go have brunch now with my friends. Good luck." I stare at the cryptic message. *You fucking child*, I want to scream. *This is not a game.*

Instead I click my phone dark, pick Louisa up off the bed, and walk around the apartment in tight circles until my parents get back.

"We should leave," I sputter as they walk through the door. I tell them about the Croatian's messages. "She said they didn't have sex," I say nervously.

"She's lying," my dad replies. "She's a horrible person. She's immoral." His voice rises louder and louder. "She knew he had a wife and newborn baby. They're both horrible people, and they're both lying to you, Jen."

"I don't know." I fidget with my sleeve. "I just want to go."

My dad calls a local U-Haul location and reserves a truck for tomorrow. We wait until Marco has left for work and then the four of us march toward my apartment. My dad splits off and takes the Subaru to the Home Depot to get some moving boxes. I pass Louisa to my mom and turn into the Rite Aid to buy formula. Louisa has begun to erupt into screams as soon as I pull her from my breast, and I am no longer confident that I am producing any milk. As I stand in line to pay, a buzzing starts in my ears. My limbs feel so heavy. There is a thick blanket of fog that is making its way through my body and it feels nice. "Wake up," I say to myself. I dig my fingernail into soft arm flesh. I barely feel anything. I am sure. I am absolutely positive that this is a dream! I have a delicious feeling suddenly that I am going to wake up at any moment. "Oh, please, please, *please wake up*," I scream to my brain. I approach the cashier.

"$10.56." The young peroxide-blonde cashier glares at me. I have a five-dollar bill and a wad of ones. I stare at the ones. I am never, ever going to be able to count to six. I don't know what to do so I hand over all my money and smile.

She looks at me curiously and counts the money methodically, handing me back two ones and a handful of change.

"Oh, whoops." I laugh as if we're sharing a joke, but it comes out strangled. She looks at me again and then says, "Next."

My whole body now feels as though it is filled with cement. I walk the block to my apartment very slowly, carefully placing one foot in front of the other, marveling at the laces on my boots. *None of this is real,* I think, and let out that strangled sound again.

My mom and I start to pack up my apartment. I am not sure how much time has passed, but my mom is putting her hand on my shoulder. I am staring at Marco's side of the closet, and I'm not sure how I got here or how long I've been staring.

"Jenny?" my mom says softly. "Why don't you gather your passport and Louisa's birth certificate. Any important documents. OK? That's all you need to focus on. Dad and I will take care of everything else."

"OK," I say back.

I watch my parents through glazed eyes. Why are they moving in slow motion? I look around my apartment. The apartment I have shared with Marco for three years. I hear my dad ask my mom, "What about those?" pointing to the four Christmas figurines lined up on the side table in the hallway. One for me, Marco, Seb, and Louisa.

"Oh, those are our first family Christmas ornaments. Marco's mom gave them to us. We'll put them on the tree again next year," I almost say, and then stop myself.

I hear my mom whisper, "Just leave them. She doesn't need those. We have plenty of ornaments at home."

I trudge slowly down the hallway into the living room. "I'm so sorry," I say blankly. "I have to go." I go to take Louisa from her bassinet.

My mom steps in front of me and says gently, "We'll bring Louisa over in a bit. We have the formula." She places her hands on my shoulders. "Can you walk back to our apartment?"

"Oh, yes, of course," I say, and open the door.

"Jen . . . do you want to put on your coat and shoes?" my mom asks, like it is the most natural question in the world.

"Oh, yes, of course," I say again. *Buzzzzzzzzzz,* I hear as I lace up my boots and zip up my big down coat. As I walk to my parents' sublet, I focus on pulling my coat zipper up and down, up and down. I have never noticed it in such detail before, and it is fascinating. It slides so easily up and down, up and down. The teeth and the zipper fit together so perfectly. Suddenly, I am standing at the front door of the sublet.

I rummage in my pocket for the keys. I stare at the keychain and then at the lock. Oh dear. I could have sworn I have unlocked this door a dozen times, but looking from the keys to the lock now, I realize that it makes absolutely no sense. There is no way that any of these keys will fit this lock. In fact, suddenly I can't tell the difference between the four different keys. They are metal with teeth and they all look the same. I decide to try every key in the lock. I am about to give up when the door clicks open.

"Yes," I say out loud, and draw out the *ssss*. That's a nice sound. "Sssssssssssssss," I say again. I am so tired and it would feel so good to sleep. I smile to myself and walk to the bed. My head hits the pillow. Sleep.

———

THE next morning, my parents wake up with a purpose. They are dressed and heading out the door to load the U-Haul as I stare up at the white ceiling from bed.

"I'll text you when we're almost done loading everything," my mom calls to me as they walk out the door. I am bringing Louisa over to say good-bye to Marco. My dad will drive the U-Haul to Maine, and my mom, Louisa, and I will follow behind him in the Subaru.

I stare at the ceiling for a few minutes longer and then stretch my arms and legs and fold my body into a sitting position.

"Hi, Lulu." She stares at me from her swing. "We're starting a new life today," I tell her with a chipper smile, and then turn away and cry. I wash my face and get dressed, change Louisa, and slip her into a fresh onesie and tiny gray leggings.

"Ready," my mom texts.

I carry Louisa in her car seat down to the lobby. I click her into the waiting stroller, and we roll toward the front doors. The glass doors framed with metal are heavy, and I clumsily open one and shove the stroller through, but it gets caught on the protruding doorframe. A woman coming down the block runs to hold the door open for me.

"Oh, thank you, thank you so much," I say gratefully, and pop the wheels of the stroller up over the ledge.

"Oh my God, she's beautiful. Look at those cheeks. Look at those eyes," the woman exclaims. "Enjoy her," she calls after me.

When I near my apartment, my parents are lifting a chair into the U-Haul.

"I think that's it," my dad tells my mom.

"Did Marco help?" I ask as I approach them.

"No. He's sleeping," my dad says briskly. "I'll go get him. If you really want to say good-bye to him."

"Yes, Dad, please. I have to."

My dad runs back in the building, and I push Louisa to the end of the block. I need to do this alone. A few minutes go by and then I see Marco appear in the doorframe wearing a white T-shirt and gray sweatpants. He looks down to where Louisa and I are waiting and disappears back inside.

"He went back in. The jerk went back in," I hear my dad say to my mom.

When he appears again, he is wearing a sweater, and he walks down the steps and moves toward us with his hands in his pockets.

I stand very still. When he reaches us, he keeps his eyes on the sidewalk. He looks into the stroller. He pats Louisa once on the head. He does not look at me. He does not say a word. He turns around and starts to walk back.

"Marco?" I say. I hate him. I hate him, and my heart is going to explode. I reach into my coat pocket and take out my engagement ring and wedding band. "I don't want these," I say.

"I don't want them either," he says.

"Take them. Take them," I yell, and yank his hand out and shove the rings into his palm. He opens his palm and my rings fall to the sidewalk and clatter. My rings are on the dirty sidewalk. Every bone in my body resists bending down, showing any weakness, but I am on my knees now, on the sidewalk, panting and picking up my rings.

I push Louisa back to the front of our old building where my mom is waiting. Marco watches passively from the building stoop.

"Let's go," I tell my mom.

"Jenny? Are you OK?" She looks at me in alarm.

"He threw my rings, Mom," I whisper, stricken. "He threw my rings on the ground. Please let's just go." But she is running back to the stoop now.

"What is wrong with you?" she screams at Marco. She climbs the steps and gets right in his face. I have never heard this voice; it is the voice of a wild animal.

Marco does not flinch. "I don't need the rings," he says flatly.

"What the hell is wrong with you?"

"I don't know, Maggie. I don't know." He folds his arms across his chest casually.

"Motherfucker." My mom spits the word at him.

"Mom, let's go. He's not worth it." My voice comes in a desperate whinny. "I hate you," I scream at Marco. My mom walks swiftly back to me and puts her arm around my shoulders. I lean half into her and half into the stroller and somehow we make it to the car.

We click Louisa into the car seat base as my dad pulls up alongside us in the U-Haul.

"Ready?" my dad asks through the window.

"Yes," I say shakily. I climb into the passenger seat, and my mom starts the car. There is a buzz and a chime, and, as I reach for my phone, I see my mom and dad also feeling for their cells.

"Do you know what it's like to say good-bye to your wife and baby and feel nothing?" the text reads. "Life is no longer worth living. I'm ending this now. Please tell Louisa that her father was very sick. I have left two letters in the apartment. One for Sebastian and one for Louisa. Please make sure they get them. I want you to know that I do love you so much, and I'm sorry I wasn't stronger. Good-bye."

As I'm reading his words, my mom says, "I just got a text from Marco that says 'I'm sorry I wasn't stronger. I'm ending it now. Good-bye.'" I jump out of the car, but somehow my mom is already in front of me, heading me off. She catches me in her arms and holds me there. "No, Jenny, no, I can't let you go back there."

"I have to stop him. I have to help him."

"Call 911. You can't go back there, Jenny. Marco is not himself right now. He's not stable." Her voice is calm and steady. "Louisa needs you." I hear Louisa screaming from the backseat.

"Yes. OK. You're right," I say, already dialing 911. I tell the operator that my husband may be attempting suicide and give her our address. She sounds bored and says there's an ambulance on the way. *Please, please let me be in time,* I pray. I hang up with 911 and dial Marco's cell phone. It rings and rings. I imagine him in the apartment. He has a knife, and he is slicing into his wrists. Blood pours into the sink. He needs me, and I am not there. I shut my eyes tightly, paralyzed inside my body. I am failing him, and I am failing Louisa by not being able to save her father. I wait five minutes and dial again. This time a strange, deep voice answers. "Hello?" I say, confused and disoriented by the foreign voice on the other end.

"Hello? This is a paramedic. Who is this?"

"Oh my God. Oh my God. Is he OK? Please, is he OK?" is all I can get out. And then, "This is his wife. I called 911."

"Well," the paramedic says sternly, "ma'am your husband was trying to kill himself. We found him with his head in the oven." Oh my God. Oh my God.

"He's OK? But he's OK?" My voice is so shrill that I worry he can't make out what I am saying.

"Yes. He's OK. We're loading him into the ambulance now. We'll be taking him to the psych ward at Elmhurst Hospital Center. You can call there in a few hours to find out more information and if he was admitted or not."

"He's OK," I scream to my mom, even though she is right beside me.

"Thank you," I say to the paramedic. "Thank you so much." I hang up.

"Jenny. Jenny. Breathe. Jenny. *You have to breathe,*" my mom is yelling. She reaches over me and opens the glove compartment. She fishes out a bag and hands it to me. *"Breathe,"* she says again.

As my mom pulls out into the street, rubbing my back with one hand and steering with the other, I bend over, my head between my knees, gulping air through a bag. He's OK. He's OK. He's OK.

———

"THE heat is so much better in there. Always has been," my mom says a few hours into the drive.

"Heat?" I repeat.

"Yes, the heat in Stella's room. You and Louisa will stay in Stella's room."

"OK." I stare straight ahead at the endless highway. My eyes glaze and my mouth falls just the tiniest bit slack, but inside my brain is working out the most complicated equation. If I can just add everything up, if I can just lay out all the pieces in my mind, starting from January 20 up until this morning, then everything will make sense. *Think. Think. You have to think about this very carefully, Jenny, if you want to figure it out.*

"Jen?" A voice nudges its way into my equation. No. No. No. I was so close to figuring everything out. Hold on, hold on to your thoughts.

"Jenny?" That voice again. Dammit. So close. So close. January 20. Croatian. Psych ward. I almost had it figured out.

"Jen." My mom yells her way into my brain, and the intricate equation in my mind breaks into a million pieces.

"Hmm?"

"I asked if you wanted to stop at the rest stop a few times. I need you to stay with me, OK?" My mom places her hand over my hand.

"Mmmm," I hum back. The problem is that Marco had his head in the oven. That is the problem. And the solution is . . . oh no. "I almost figured it out," I say softly.

"Figured what out?" my mom asks.

"Everything." Everything, everything, everything.

BEFORE

"You lost a little more blood than we'd like, so we're going to keep monitoring your blood pressure, OK?" The doctor peeled red gloves from her hands. "Nothing major but outside the normal range. I gave you a shot to help you clot, and we're going to keep an eye on your blood pressure for the next couple of days just to be safe."

"Was that the shot directly into my butt?" I said, and tried to give a wry smile. I turned my head to look at Louisa. The nurse was taking her measurements on a table across the room.

"That was the one. Fun, huh?" The doctor smiled.

"I barely felt it," I said. I wanted to ask some questions, but I felt too weak and closed my eyes instead.

A nurse came over and said, "I'm going to press on your stomach. We want to get any clots and extra blood out, OK?" I nodded, and she placed two large hands on my stomach and pushed down hard. "Oooooh," was the only noise I could make. I felt a river of blood come flowing out of me and then heard it splash on the floor.

"OK, honey, so that was a lot that just came out. I'm going to take your blood pressure right now, OK?"

I nodded again. "Marco," I whispered, and held out my hand. He put his phone into his pocket and held my hand. "You're fine, baby. This is all normal."

"Hmm," the nurse said as the cuff loosened around my arm. "It's a little low but not too bad. I'll take it again in an hour. You should be fine to go into a recovery room. Hey, Dad"—the nurse looked to Marco—"do you two have a private recovery room?"

Marco put away his phone again and looked at the nurse blankly.

"We're on the waiting list for a private room," I said from the chair. "The front desk lady said all the private rooms were occupied when we were admitted but to check with her when we were actually going to our room for the night."

"I'll go check," Marco said quickly, and left the room.

"What happens if there's no private rooms?" I asked the nurse.

"Then you share a room with someone else and Hubby gets to go home for the night," she said with a small laugh. I felt the rest of the blood drain from my face.

Marco walked back in the room, and the nurse and I looked at him expectantly. "She said there are still no private rooms tonight but there might be one tomorrow night." He looked up from his phone. "Having a work crisis anyway, so I'll just go straight to work after you and the baby get settled."

I tried to catch Marco's eyes to show him that I needed him. "I really don't want to be alone tonight," I whispered.

"I know, baby." Marco took my hand. "But it's just one night and then I'll be with you guys tomorrow night."

The nurse brought a wheelchair into the room, and Marco and she lifted me into it. Another nurse placed a sleeping Louisa, wrapped up in a blanket like a tiny burrito, into my arms. Marco pushed me out of the room into the hallway. "Babe?" I said. "Can you get my parents from the waiting room?"

I stared into the tiny red face while I waited for my parents and Marco. "Hello," I said tentatively.

"There they are! There they are!" I heard my mom's excited voice drift down the hallway. I smiled as my parents approached and felt tears stream down my cheeks. "Meet Louisa Evelyn Medina," I said proudly.

"Louisa," my mom echoed, and peered down at the sleeping baby in my arms. "Yes, she's a Louisa," she said, pulling out two tissues from her pocket, one for each of us.

"How do you feel, Jenny?" my dad asked. "You look very pale."

"I'm OK." I half smiled. "Just feel a little weak." I looked down the hallway. "Wait, where's Marco?"

"He's on a work call," my mom said.

"He said there's some kind of emergency at work. He seemed pretty stressed out," my dad added.

Just then the nurse who pressed on my stomach came briskly around the corner. "There you are!" she called. "You come with me," she said with her Jamaican lilt. "I just saw an empty private room, so we're going to take it!" she said happily.

I broke into a huge smile. "Really? Is that allowed?"

"It is now," she said, pushing me with determination toward the recovery wing.

We passed Marco on the way, and I called to him, "She found us a private room! We're going there now!" Marco cradled his phone into his neck and gave us two thumbs up as we hurried by.

A FEW hours later I sat with a lactation consultant and grimaced in pain as Louisa bobbed around and then latched on to my nipple. "Oh no, no," the white-haired consultant clucked calmly, "that's a cheap latch." She unsuctioned Louisa gently with her finger. "Let's try again. She's got a really powerful suck. You want to get her used to a wide latch, otherwise you'll be in a lot of pain later." It was around 9:00 P.M., and I had been trying to get Louisa to eat for the past hour. My parents had gone home for the night, and Marco was in the hallway on the phone again.

Marco ducked his head into the room. "Hey, babe, I have to run to the restaurant. We had two guys call out sick tonight. I'll be quick. I just need to see what's going on and help out during the rush. An hour, tops." He smiled at the white-haired lady, and she smiled back.

"OK, sure." I tried to keep my voice steady. "Please hurry back."

As soon as the lactation consultant left, Louisa began to cry. Softly at first and then louder and louder. Her tinny wails filled the room and seemed to build with each cry. I heaved myself off the bed. *I can do this,* I told myself. *I'm her mother; I can figure this out.* I walked the ten steps from one side of the room to the other,

bouncing her in my arms. I swayed her from side to side. I *shhhh
shhhh shhhhhh*ed over and over. I paced the room until I felt dizzy
and had to sit down on the bed. I jiggled her in my arms on the
bed. I looked at the clock. It was 11:00 P.M. Marco had been gone
for two hours. I placed her crumpled face against my nipple, hoping she'd latch on. I took her out of the swaddle and wrapped her
up again. Nothing worked. I felt an unfocused sense of panic
coursing through my veins. Sweat trickled down my sides and
thighs. She was never going to stop crying. I got back up and
walked in tight circles around the room, my panic mounting with
each wail. I glanced at the clock. Midnight. Finally, I picked up my
phone from the side table.

"FUCK YOU," I shot off to Marco. I had never said or written those words to my husband, and I immediately felt a pang of
regret.

"I didn't do anything wrong?!?" came Marco's reply instantly.

"Where are you? I can't do this," I wrote back, and then started
to cry.

"Still at work. Be there soon."

Finally, I pressed the call button. A nurse walked in a few
minutes later. "What's going on in here?" she said, taking in the
scene with a sympathetic smile.

"She's been crying for hours. I've tried everything."

"Do you have a partner to help out tonight?" The nurse
looked around the tiny room.

"My husband should be back soon. He had to work." My voice
broke, and tears streamed down my face. "I just can't make her stop
crying. I don't know what to do."

The nurse took over and swaddled Louisa so tightly in the

blanket that I asked, "Are you sure she can breathe like that?" But it worked. Louisa gave one final cry and then, like magic, fell asleep immediately. Exhausted and grateful, I also closed my eyes and sank into the reclined chair.

An hour later, I heard the door open and footsteps shuffle into the room. I waited for Marco to come to me, but he carefully navigated his way to the pullout couch, took off his shoes, and laid down.

AFTER

MARCO gets out of the hospital today. I am sitting on the couch, holding my knees and rocking back and forth. Nat told me yesterday that when she went to the hospital to drop off pajamas for Marco, she glanced through the sign-in sheet discreetly. The Croatian had been there every single day, multiple times a day.

"Jenny?" my mom says. "What's going on? What are you thinking right now?"

"Marco gets out today," I say in a nervous whisper. "I know, I just know that they're going to have sex tonight. They're finally going to," I say, staring straight ahead. I bite my thumbnail and continue to rock.

"Oh, Jenny," my mom says softly. I think she's going to reluctantly agree. I brace myself. She comes and sits beside me on the couch. She tucks a long strand of hair behind my ear. "Oh, honey, they've already had sex."

My head snaps to look at her. I see pity in her eyes as I realize that I am the very last person now to understand. "But . . . ," I say, "she confirmed it was an emotional affair. She said 'you know everything now' and that they didn't have sex." My mom looks at me sadly.

"Honey, a man doesn't leave his beautiful wife and newborn baby for an emotional affair. For talking. And a girl like that doesn't have an emotional affair." My mom bounces Louisa on her knees. "I'm so sorry. I know this is hard for you to hear."

"But how do you know?" I ask. "How do you know for sure?"

My mom hesitates and then says simply, "The bed."

"The bed? What are you talking—" I stop speaking as every-thing clicks into place in my brain. "The bed," I say again. This time it is not a question.

I can't bring myself to discuss this shard of the puzzle quite yet. So I say, "Of course you're right." I stand up. "I just need to go upstairs for a minute." I walk from the room quickly as my mom calls "Jenny" after me. I take the stairs to my bedroom two at a time. I climb onto my bed as my face collapses. I hear an animal wailing. It sounds like it is being tortured. I am vaguely concerned before I realize that the sound is coming from me. My dad is climbing onto my bed before I even know he is in the room. My dad, who shakes his own siblings' hands firmly at family gather-ings to avoid personal contact; my dad, who has not seen me cry since the age of nine when I skinned my knee sliding into home base, wraps his arms tightly around me, and I fall into his chest. He holds me while I sob and wail. Finally, as my noises start to quiet into small gasps, he speaks over my hair. "You're going to have to decide. Not right now. But someday, you're going to have to decide not to care about him anymore. As long as you still care, he can hurt you."

"But, Dad," I start to say.

"I know. I know," he says, anticipating my protests. "It's going to be hard. It's going to be extremely difficult. It's going to take a long time. It might take a few months. It might take a few years. Probably it will be somewhere in between. You were married. You have a baby. But at some point, you will have to make a decision."

I try to hear his words. I try to take in his advice. My dad always gives good, practical advice. I know, even now, hunched against his chest, that I will have to take his advice someday. But all I can manage to say is, "I don't know. I just don't know."

"I love you," he says, and kisses my head.

"I love you, too. I'll be down soon." My dad's arms release their grip. The bed creaks. He closes my bedroom door behind him. Suddenly, I am exhausted. Just as my eyes are closing, my phone lights up on the bedside table. I see the name "Marco" from the corner of my eye and snatch my phone off the table. My heart is in my throat as I imagine what his first communication to me will be after his suicide attempt. Maybe, just maybe, with five days alone to think in the hospital . . .

I swipe the text open.

"I'm sorry to bother you, but what are we doing for bills this month?"

————

A HUNDRED times a day there is a voice in my head that screams *Help me*. The voice comes from a tiny woman in my chest encased in a soundproof glass column, pounding on the walls, begging for someone to notice her. When I look at the one picture from our city hall wedding that I still have in my phone, the tiny woman goes crazy, her fists beating against the glass over and over again. But I keep her locked inside my chest; the only sign of her existence is the lump that I swallow down as I zoom in on our radiant, bursting-with-happiness faces. She is the reason I can't leave the house for more than two hours. She is the reason my face will suddenly become very still, causing my mom to ask, "Jenny?"

"I don't feel well," I say to my parents, and wherever we are, whatever we are doing, we silently pack up and leave, a quick, clean exit.

"How are you feeling?" they ask me on the way home, glancing into the rearview mirror.

"I'm OK. I just don't feel good," I say, and lean my head into the car door. I don't have the energy to explain that there is a battle raging inside me. I go through the motions with Louisa, but I don't really see her. I nurse her, I change her, I hold her. But I can't see her clearly. She is blurry, like the space inside my head now. There is a fog that follows me wherever I go. It is thick, and I long to break through to the other side, but sometimes I find myself clinging to it, laying my head in its warm, fuzzy lap, and letting it lull me to sleep. I don't know how I get through the days. The moments string together to become hours, and somehow suddenly it is 6:00 P.M. and I am nursing Louisa to sleep.

Every day I wake up to Louisa's cries. I pull myself into a sitting position. My head throbs. I sit for a moment and think about where I am and what happened. "I am in Maine with my three-month-old baby living with my parents. My husband is in our home in New York, and he has a twenty-two-year-old Croatian girlfriend." I repeat this in my head until it sinks in or until

Louisa's cries drown it out. One leg swings over the side of the bed followed by the other. I don't know how they move, but they do. I reach down and pick up Louisa. I make soft, sweet sounds. I bring her into my bed and nurse her. I try to feel love and warmth, but I feel nothing. I text "nursing, be done soon," to my mom. I stare at the white wall across from my bed and think, *I am nursing our baby, and my husband is with his twenty-two-year-old Croatian girlfriend.* I stroke Louisa's hair and think, *Marco. Marco. Marco.*

I hear footsteps on the stairs, and then my mom is peering into the room. She smiles at me, and the corners of my mouth turn up.

"Thank you," I say as she takes Louisa.

"Try to sleep," she says, and leaves. She sings to Louisa on the way downstairs.

I lay my head down on my pillow. I close my eyes, but I do not sleep. How could my Marco do this? Did my subconscious know the whole time? Is that why every once in a while I would dream that I had lost him? What happened to my sweet husband, trudging into the living room in flannel pajamas, his hair sticking up all over his head, flopping down next to me on the couch, squeezing his face against mine until I yell, "Your bristles, babe—ouch!"

I open my eyes and swing my legs to the floor again. I walk to the bathroom. I brush my teeth. I walk down the stairs, past the nook where Marco proposed, and into the family room. I turn my mouth up again when I see my mom and Louisa. I nurse her. My mom sits on the couch across from me and asks how I am and if I slept OK. "Yes, thank you," I say. I give Louisa back to my mom and walk back upstairs. I turn on the shower and step in. I sit down on the floor and hug my knees. My tears and snot run down the drain. *How?* I think over and over. *How did you do this?* By the time I turn the knob all the way to the left and the water stops, my face is red and raw. I towel off and then carefully apply makeup in the mirror. I check my phone to see if Marco has texted me. I go back downstairs and sit on the couch and watch my parents with Louisa. I think, *Thank God, thank God for my parents.* My mom asks if I want to take a walk. We walk around the loop, my mom pushing the bright red stroller, and she tells me, "He tried really hard for five years, Jenny. He tried really hard to be someone he's not, and finally he just couldn't do it anymore. You have to start thinking of him as a deeply, deeply flawed person who tried his best and failed."

The hours blur together. In the back of my mind there is always the thought, *How? How did you do this, Marco? I needed you. I needed you. I needed you.* At 6:00 P.M. I start getting Louisa's tubby ready. I stand over her at the sink, cupping my hands with water and releasing it onto her body in streams. "Good girl," I say, and when she splashes and gurgles for the first time, the dull ache that is always there turns into a thousand sharp knives piercing my insides, and I think, *You're missing this, Marco.* I wrap her in a towel and bring her upstairs. I put one arm and then the other into her PJ sleeves. I do the snaps as she squiggles. I nurse her until her eyes start to close, and then I let the hot, salty liquid fall from my eyes. I blot her hair dry with a tissue before I lower her into her swing.

Holly is home, and she's coming over tonight. When my parents tell me this, I think, *Why is she home?* But it is a distant, vague thought, and it crumbles and dissolves quickly.

"J," she says when she walks in the door, "I know we both have personal space issues, but I'm going to hug you."

"Totally legit," I say, and crack a smile. I don't know how to talk about the mess inside my head, so I ask her about New York, auditions, Mike. It has been only a few minutes, but this is the longest I've talked to someone about "normal" things since I got home, and I realize very quickly that I can't do it. There is a tidal wave in my chest and it is rising, rising and it is going to crash and my ears start to buzz and my vision becomes blurry. I try to focus on a magazine on the coffee table in front of us, but I can no longer form words and then I am sputtering, "I can't. I'm sorry. I can't be normal." Holly is next to me; she wraps her arms around me, and I collapse into her. She is crying too, and I say, "Don't cry," and she says, "You don't deserve this," and even though my head is full of wet cotton I think very clearly, *What an innocent thing to say.*

The girl who believed that good or bad things happen because you deserve them is long gone.

———

MARCO'S parents flew to New York yesterday from Denmark. I have been in constant communication with Sofia since the day I left New York.

"My dad sits and stares, and my mom just cries and cries," she whispered to me during a late-night phone call. "They are flying to New York as soon as possible. They want to be by Marco's side."

Secretly, I am hoping that they will prevent Marco from spending time with the Croatian. I spend my days robotically caring for Louisa and obsessively checking her Instagram account. The day after Marco was released from the hospital, she posted a picture from inside the trendy, old-fashioned barbershop a block from our apartment. "First trip to the barbershop!" the caption read. During the last months of my pregnancy, Marco started frequenting that barbershop more and more. Only now do I connect the dots between his mounting obsession with his hair and the start of his affair. We walked there every two weeks, hand in hand, my swollen belly leading the way. He kissed me outside the shop before I continued on my way to do the grocery shopping or run errands. "My pretty husband," I'd teased him before waddling away.

"Sofia, I hope your parents understand what they're in for," I whispered back, telling her about the girl's picture.

"Don't worry, *mi amor,* my dad will talk sense into Marco. He is a grown man, but my parents won't stand for him carrying on this relationship."

I've also started talking more and more with Seb's mom. As the person in the United States who has known Marco the longest, I am holding out hope that one day she will help me figure out exactly what happened. "Aha, I forgot to tell you this pertinent piece of information that will explain how Marco went from being madly in love with you to sneaking around with his twenty-two-year-old girlfriend right after you gave birth to his baby," she will say. So far, no dice. Her only, and best, theory is a brain tumor. There is a large part of me that wishes this to be true.

"I always knew he could be a bit dense sometimes and immature, but I thought he was basically a good person," she texts. "I didn't think he was a lying, cheating, Croella-fucking asshole."

Nat and her boyfriend started calling the Croatian "Croella," for Croatian Cruella de Vil, because of her blackened eyebrows and obsession with fur coats. The name has stuck. I refresh her Instagram profile dozens of times a day, sick to my stomach with fear and anticipation of her next photo. She posts multiple selfies a day, and all of her photos now seem to be not-so-subtle digs or clues that she's with Marco, such as the barbershop photo.

"Does she really have to fuck your husband while you have stitches in your vagina and then kick you while you're down? Doesn't she have the decency to at least be ashamed?" Nat texts me as the pictures come in.

I walk with my mom and Louisa around and around the loop, talking through everything, still trying to make sense of everything that has happened since January 20. When I feel the familiar tightening of my chest, I head back home, and my mom continues on with Louisa. Sometimes, when Lulu cries and cries, refusing to fall asleep, my parents and I take turns holding her, sliding around briskly in our socks on the hardwood floor of the kitchen, hoping the motion will lull her to sleep. Sometimes, when the anxiety mounts and my heart feels like it's going to explode, my parents take turns without me.

The anxiety comes in waves now. Some moments, even some hours, I am fine. Other times I am paralyzed by anxiety and depression and anger. I can't think. I can't feel. All I hear is a buzzing inside my head drowning out everything else. My limbs feel so heavy that lifting my daughter seems almost impossible. But I do it anyway. Because what other choice do I have? I take deep breaths. I have to keep breathing. If I focus on breathing I can undo the knot in my stomach enough so that I can keep going. But secretly I wonder, will I ever be OK? Is this a test that I am going to fail? What if I find out that I am actually not strong enough? That the person revealed will be a shriveling, shaking, scared little girl? My daughter whimpers at the toy just out of her reach, and I am shocked back to life. Suddenly, I am on my feet, moving toward her, and the room comes into focus as I bend over her and turn my lips to a smile. I have made it through another panic attack.

BEFORE

"DON'T cry, baby, please don't cry," Marco said to me, half asleep as I kissed him good-bye. "I'm going to miss you guys so much."

"I don't know why I'm crying. It must be hormones," I said, gasping through a sob. "It's only ten days," I added, and kissed him again. Louisa and I were leaving for Maine with my parents since Marco's boss was on vacation for the next two weeks. Marco would be working double-duty and was worried that he wouldn't be able to help at all at home. When my parents told us that they were going to check on the house in Maine and return for my sister's birthday, Marco had insisted that Louisa and I go with them.

"I love you." He closed his eyes.

"I love you so."

The first days in Maine with Louisa were bad. She cried day and night. When she wasn't crying, I anxiously tiptoed around, dreading the moment she would wake and start up again. Stella came over the third day we were home with a mechanical swing in tow. She lugged it into our parents' house and triumphantly plopped it down in the living room.

"This worked every time with Henry. When he was really fussy and nothing else would work, this was the only thing that would guarantee sleep." She plugged in the swing and hit the number 5 on the side panel. The numbers went up to eight. "Don't bother with anything lower than four," she said, snatching a wailing Louisa from my arms. She bounced Lulu for a moment on her six-months-pregnant belly and then lowered her gently into the swing. We waited as the swing gained speed.

"Are you sure it's not going too fast?" I asked, my eyes transfixed on Lulu.

"It's fine," Stella replied. "It goes up to eight for a reason." She stared at Lulu, too. We both waited. The swing went faster and faster. Suddenly, Louisa's screams began to quiet, and her eyes began to flicker closed.

"Oh my God," I whispered. "The swing."

"See," Stella whispered back, staring at Lulu. "Miracle worker. Worked on Henry every—"

Just then a wail ripped out of Louisa, and her eyes opened. Her face crumpled, and shrieks filled the air.

"Oh no," I said numbly. Tears streamed down my face. "It didn't work."

Stella crossed her arms. "Fuck."

"Thanks for trying," I said, scooping Louisa from the swing. "I just don't know what to do about sleep. I haven't slept in so long. She wakes up every hour or two hours and sometimes she cries for hours and at night, it's so much harder and God, I just wish Marco were here—"

"You need to get more than an hour of uninterrupted sleep, Jenny," Stella cut in. "Mom, Dad," she yelled into the family room. "I'm going to tell them to take turns with Lulu until midnight tonight. You go to bed at six. OK?"

"No, I can't ask them to do that, Stella! They've already helped so—"

"This is not up for debate," Stella said, cutting me off again. "*Mom! Dad!*"

That night I slept for five hours. Around midnight I woke to footsteps on the stairs and wailing. A soft knock and then, "Jenny?" My mom opened the door and brought Louisa in. "I'm so sorry, I really wanted to get her to sleep before I brought her up, but she's having a rough night."

I rubbed my eyes and leaped out of bed, my drunken stupor of sleep was already replaced by adrenaline pumping through my blood from hearing Louisa's cries. "It's OK," I said. "Thank you so much."

"Good luck, honey," my mom said, giving us one last worried look and closing the bedroom door.

The rest of the week felt like an eternity. "I need to come home," I told Marco on the phone at the end of the week. "I'm going to see if we can leave today instead of tomorrow. I can't do this without you."

"Babe, calm down, I promise you can do this." Marco's voice, husky with sleep, filled my ear. "You're the strongest person I know. Just one more night. You can do this."

"I don't know." I closed my eyes and took a deep breath. "Just talking to you is making me feel better though," I said. "How are things in New York? How is work?"

"Honestly, it's awful, baby. Even if you came back tonight, I wouldn't be home till four A.M. My boss is still on vacation, and I've been spending seriously sixteen hours a day at the restaurant. It's insanity."

"God, I guess we're both equally sleep deprived." I gave a dry laugh. "Why do people have children again?"

"Legacy, continuing the bloodline, not having to die alone, all that," Marco said. "Shit, babe, it's noon. I gotta get ready for work. I'll see you guys tomorrow, OK? I can't wait. I miss you so much."

"I miss you, too."

"Wait, babe? Can you text me when you leave tomorrow? So that I make sure that I'm home when you guys get back?"

"Of course."

"Oh, babe! One more thing!"

"Yes?" I laugh into the phone.

"Remind me to tell you something about the bed. It's not a big deal at all. Don't worry."

"OK, crazy pants." I yawn big. "Anything else?"

"I love you."

"I love you so."

AFTER

TODAY I wake up, and instead of checking Marco's Facebook and the Croatian's Instagram, I Google "husband affair liar
personality change." I click one of the first websites that pops up.
It is all about different types of lying. I read about compulsive
(mindless, automatic lying) versus pathological (intentionally de-
ceitful and self-serving lying) and white lies (lies that we all tell at
one point or another) versus destructive lies (lies with the intent
to hurt or deceive another). Marco is definitely a pathological liar,
of that I am certain. It feels good to put a name to his specific type
of lying, and I feel the tiniest bit of power seep back into my body
as I scroll. Next I Google "pathological liars" and "my husband is
a pathological liar," and I read everything I can about these types
of liars. Many of the articles advise that intense therapy may help
a pathological liar but that even with a lot of therapy it is a long
shot. Often these liars don't want to be helped and will lie to the

therapist. I read another excerpt that says if your partner has lied to you about something as serious as cheating, your finances, or an addiction, you may give him an hour or two, or at the most twenty-four hours, to come clean, and if he does not, then he has made the decision for you to end the relationship. I read that line again and again. He has made the decision for you to end the relationship because he has chosen that there will be no respect, openness, or true intimacy in the relationship.

Ha, I think, *twenty-four hours?* I gave Marco an entire month in my confused, hormonal state. I let myself believe that he was suffering from burnout and spent hours researching symptoms and treatment, knowing deep in my stomach that something didn't add up but terrified of failing my husband in his time of need. "Lying piece of shit," I mutter to myself, and keep reading. The next article I click on is a psychologist responding to a woman who says she has been married to a pathological liar for twelve years. She desperately wants him to stop lying, but she has no idea what to do. The psychologist prescribes counseling and warns that the best route may be simply to leave and limit contact with her husband. In the last part of his response he says, *"There is one type of pathological liar that I cannot in good conscience advise you to stay with under any circumstance and that is the sociopath. The sociopath cannot and will not change because he does not have a conscience. Your only recourse if you determine that your husband suffers from this personality disorder is to distance yourself from him and limit contact immediately or better yet go no contact."* I feel my blood turn to ice. Sociopath. I've heard the word before in the news relating to murderers and rapists, but I always thought of sociopaths like Santa Claus, prolific in stories but not in real life.

I Google "What is a sociopath" and bring up the first link. My breath comes in short, shallow spurts as I read the first paragraph on the screen. I read that sociopaths are not just murderers. They can be your neighbor, your coworker, a family member, or even your soul mate. In fact, many people who never used or believed in the term "soul mate" before use that exact word to describe their sociopathic partners. I think back to all the times I gushed to my friends and family, "I've never felt this way before. I don't even believe in soul mates but I really think Marco is my soul mate!" My stomach flips and flops, and I keep reading. The article goes on to say that defining a sociopath is more complex than one may think; there is no one single trait used to "diagnose" a sociopath; rather, it is a personality disorder with a cluster of related symptoms. Because there are many traits used to classify a sociopath an individual must possess a majority of certain behaviors to fall somewhere in the wide spectrum of the disorder. My eyes quickly scan to find the criteria, or red flags, of a sociopath. As I read each trait, my heart beats faster, and the hair on my arms rises. Charming. Check. Impulsive. Check. No remorse, guilt, or shame. Check. Invents lies. Speaks poetically. Incapable of apologizing. Check, check, check. Before I delve further into my research, I hear Louisa waking from her nap next door.

As I nurse Lulu my mind spins. Marco can't really be a sociopath. We were together for five years, and I never saw any signs until now. Could he have really been "wearing a mask" for five years? No. It's not possible. He had a mental breakdown and an affair. His mind snapped because he was exhausted and overworked and felt so much pressure to provide. Except, the nagging voice in the back of my mind says, a "normal" man would have owned up by now and at least given some sort of apology. It has been two months since I opened our computer and saw that e-mail, and Marco continues to not only play the victim but he is . . . mean to me . . . when he is not sending me "I love you more than anything in the world" texts, that is. I know that is not "normal," but I haven't been able to put my finger on exactly why. And then I realize, he is *still* trying to play both sides. Instead of letting me go and letting me grieve, or deciding that he made the biggest mistake of his life and doing everything to win back his family, he reels me in and then casts me out on a daily basis. I spend the rest of the day pondering this. I text Nat later that night, trying to put this nagging feeling into words, and she replies, "Right. He isn't treating you like a PERSON with thoughts and feelings and needs. Even his 'lovey' texts are not actually about YOU and how he hurt YOU. They're about him and how he ruined his life. He doesn't say 'My God, I can't believe I put you through hell,' he says 'All I want is my wife back. All I want is my life.' HIS wife. HIS life. Every single thing he says relates back to HIM."

She's right. It's like I am generic cardboard cutout "wife" to him instead of a real human being.

Nat has finally put into words the feeling that I could not describe. Marco does not see me as a human being anymore.

I pick my phone back up and turn on my bedside lamp. I read about personality disorders for an hour. My eyes grow heavy and blur. I know that Louisa will be awake to nurse soon, but I can't stop. I am riveted. I finally feel a sense of control after spinning for months. Everything I read about sociopaths matches up with Marco's behavior in the past couple of months. One article highlights that sociopaths hate being alone. I think about Marco going straight from Tania to me and then from me to the Croatian. I remember Marco saying, "I can't be alone. You know I hate being alone," as if that was a justification for him continuing his affair. The article concludes by saying that a sociopath will repeat the same relationship cycle over and over again; lather, rinse, repeat. I Google "sociopath relationship cycle." I click a link that leads to a page with a shadowy figure wearing a mask with the words "Idealize, Devalue, Discard" on it. I have not even read what this means and chills creep all over my body. *Idealize, devalue, discard.* I know instinctively that this is exactly what has happened to me, and I devour the article and then read it three more times.

At the beginning of any relationship involving a sociopath, or psychopath (I read that the words are actually interchangeable), the victim, or target, of the sociopath is overvalued, idealized, placed on a pedestal. The sociopath has targeted this person for a reason and pursues said target with a single-mindedness that comes as close to love as a sociopath will ever feel. But it is not love, not at all. It is obsession, infatuation, a desire to possess and then destroy. Once the sociopath has zeroed in on a target and decided that she has something he wants, he will then "love bomb" her. *Love bombing* is a deluge of constant flattery and attention that may come in many different forms. This is how sociopaths seduce their targets. My fingers tremble as I scroll through this paragraph and read it again. I remember the beginning of my relationship with Marco. The constant texting, the overwhelming flattery and attention, my heightened emotional state. I remember chalking it up to "Latin charm" and feeling like the luckiest girl in the world.

Another tactic the sociopath uses is called "mirroring." The sociopath assesses his target and then reflects back to her exactly what she loves in herself and what she doesn't even know she desires in a mate. The sociopath mirrors his victim so completely that the victim truly believes she has found her soul mate, her kindred spirit, her other half. He values what she values, copies her taste in music, clothes, even friends. His long-term goals align exactly with hers, and they excitedly make plans for the future.

I think about Nat telling me that Marco became so sweet and gentle when he met me, a better father to Seb and a better man in general. She really thought we were one of those couples who made the other one a better person. He became kinder, more mature, and seemed to get his priorities straightened out, proving that the real problem that had driven them apart was his relationship with Tania, and now he was living up to his full potential. I believed that we lifted each other up and brought out the best in each other. I had found my other half in a tattooed single father living in New York City illegally for twelve years. In the least likely of people, I had found my fairy-tale ending. Is it possible that Marco was only mirroring my personality? Showing me exactly what I didn't even know I was looking for in a partner? *No,* I think quickly, *it's not possible.* This article says the average idealize phase lasts for a few months and then devaluing begins. Marco worshipped the ground I walked on for five years. I bite my thumbnail and Google "sociopath idealize lasts for years." There are not many hits that match my search. I'm reaching. Marco can't possibly be an actual sociopath. As much as I want an explanation for everything that has happened since January 20, as much as I need to make sense of my husband, my best friend, my protector fading from my life right after I gave birth, maybe there is an explanation that is far more common. He simply fell out of love and had an affair. Perhaps he is a cheater and a coward and that is all. Except I know it is not that simple. Most men who have affairs don't lie about it to the point that they would rather go to a psych ward than come clean. Most men who have affairs don't make up serious medical conditions in order to escape taking responsibility for their actions. And most men who have affairs don't choose the timing that Marco chose. The exact moment our baby was born.

I finally find an article about sociopaths who actually marry their targets and why this happens. Most often it is for a cloak of reputability, a nice backdrop against which they can live out their dark desires. The author of this article is adamant that the sociopath who marries his target cannot and will not be faithful for long, at the most a matter of months or just long enough to secure the marriage. I try to think as objectively as I can about our relationship. I imagine Marco cheating on me around the time we went to Bloomingdale's and ate frozen yogurt. I remember our city hall wedding and his dimple as he smiled at me and said "I do." I think about opening the Thirsty Owl and the nights we spent pacing around the living room. "If we can get through this, we can get through anything," he said. No, no, no. If Marco is a sociopath, then he is the only sociopath who managed to stay faithful for five years before he lost control. At the end of the article the author explains that some targets provide such large sources of ego fuel that they may remain in the idealize phase for years, depending on what the sociopath desires out of the relationship. The article calls this "narcissistic supply" and states that all sociopaths are also narcissists. I read the next line: If a target is providing a constant stream of supply, they may be overvalued and idealized by the sociopath for many years. However, when their supply eventually decreases, they will be quickly devalued and discarded. Oh my God. Green card. Restaurant. Wedding. Travel. Reputability. Maine. Money. Family. I was an almost never-ending source of supply for Marco until I had a baby and suddenly, my stock plummeted. I would no longer be feeding his ego if I was taking care of a newborn.

The next couple of paragraphs are about the devalue phase. When the target is no longer useful or providing enough narcissistic supply, the dark void that is always lurking within the sociopath opens and he starts to methodically devalue the very traits of his target he once overvalued. Did Marco devalue me? I think back over the course of our relationship. I feel as though I went from being on a pedestal to being thrown away like yesterday's trash. Is it possible to go straight from the idealize stage to being abruptly discarded?

My eyes land on a long thread called "Psychopath Fetishes," and, intrigued, I dive in. "Oh my God," I say out loud while reading. The main fetish that comes up again and again is feet, Marco's favorite. I always knew Marco had a thing for my feet, but it wasn't until recently that Nat filled me in on the scope of his foot fetish.

"Wait, I'm sorry. You were *married* to him, actually, you *are* married to him, and he never told you about his foot fetish?" she asked incredulously a couple of weeks ago.

"Well, I mean, I know he likes feet," I said. "But I guess he never really expressed to me how deeply he likes them?"

"I would say that Marco's foot fetish is his defining feature. Like, when I think of Marco, I think of his foot fetish."

Even in the dark despair and chaos of those first weeks, this information blew my mind. My husband had a fetish that defined him as a person, and he never told me? He had made several comments the first year we were dating about how he loved it when I wore heels, but, as far as I remember, nothing along the lines of "I want to suck on your toes all day and all night." Or, "I will wither away and die if I can't worship female feet." That definitely would have stuck in my mind.

"I don't find it strange that he has a foot fetish; I find it strange that he never *shared* with me that he has a foot fetish," I told Nat. "I'm pretty sure when you decide to spend the rest of your life with someone, expressing your most base desires and fantasies is important?"

In the thread, someone mentions that many psychopathic fetishes and fantasies tend to run more toward the extreme. One of the examples given is a fixation on extremely "deviant" porn. Because psychopathic personalities are characterized by having low impulse control and needing constant stimulation, many, if not all, psychopaths are sex addicts and sexual deviants. Psychopaths have no real identity; the dark void within is always lurking. They are empty creatures, and so they will engage in more and more promiscuous and extreme behavior to feel anything at all.

I keep reading, and when I see the word *vore* for the third time, I finally Google it. I read the Wikipedia article on what vore is, and I feel physically ill. Many psychopaths are preoccupied with vore, or the desire to be consumed whole, like a snake eating its victim alive in one gulp. This is a sexual fantasy that cannot be acted out in real life for obvious reasons, but it is still a sexual fixation for many psychopaths.

My mind is spinning, but now my eyes are so heavy that I can barely keep them open. I drift off to sleep and dream I am walking next to Marco on a wooden bridge high above beautiful mountains. We look down at the clouds and the green-and-brown earth below us. My dress stretches over my huge, round belly. We are laughing and holding hands. Suddenly, Marco lets go of my hand and turns toward me. His shining eyes are now dark and lifeless. "What's wrong?" I ask. His arms reach out toward me, and with one shove I am falling, falling through endless air into oblivion.

"Marco," I scream. I am crying, but not because I am scared of falling. I don't understand what I did to make Marco push me. "Marco," I try to scream again, but air rushes into my lungs and the next words get lodged in my throat: "I needed you."

———

THE next morning I walk into the kitchen with Lulu and pour myself a cup of coffee. I sit down on the couch next to my mom and say, "Did you look at the link I sent you last night?"

I tell my mom about my reading and what I've learned. I mention another article about a woman who was in the idealize phase for three years and then she had a miscarriage and was devalued and discarded while she was in the hospital. "It's like the mask drops when they are called on to be the nurturer in the relationship for once. You know, I never expressed it in words, but I think I innately felt like *Finally, it's Marco's turn to take care of me,* after I put so much into him for so long. And then instead of taking care of me, he had an affair."

We discuss this for a while, and the conversation morphs into all the tiny signs that Marco had started to devalue me that we missed. I am certain that if I can understand exactly what happened and why, I will be able to move forward. Otherwise I am afraid I will be stuck here, in this gray place, forever.

"Do you remember how uninvolved he was with getting Louisa's nursery ready?" my mom says. "And when we surprised you guys with the IKEA furniture after Thanksgiving? He almost seemed annoyed. We gave him a pass because we all thought he was working so hard."

I think back to November, the month before Louisa was born and the month that I now believe the affair started. Marco seemed to be exhausted and withdrawn much of the time, but that was because he was working nonstop, crazy hours. My parents surprised us by buying a new IKEA couch for our living room, and I remember Marco saying "It's interesting how your parents think they can just rearrange our entire apartment." I had brushed off his comment with a laugh. "You know they like to be very involved. It can be a bit much, but I don't think we can really complain. I mean, they're *moving* here for three months to help us with the baby."

"True," he said, and flicked on the TV.

"Wow, you're right." I look at my mom. "It was very subtle, but I think he was actually devaluing our entire family. He went from adoring you and idolizing Dad to being vaguely annoyed and irritated at all the help you were providing us. Jesus. This is really sad, but at the time I actually thought, *Finally, we've exited the honeymoon phase a bit after four years.* I actually thought it was more normal and healthy that he wasn't still over the moon in love and excited and happy all the time and he was getting annoyed with me once in a while."

Suddenly, I have a vivid flash to standing in the living room of our apartment in New York, holding Louisa. It was one of the mornings after we had driven back to New York City from Maine. One of the ten mornings we had to get through before packing up and moving into the cottage on Peaks Island.

"Ready to go to brunch?" I said, bouncing Louisa side to side on my hip. Marco looked at me closely and then held out his arms. "Here, I'll hold the baby while you go do your makeup."

"Oh," I had said, wounded for half a second, and then, "right, thanks."

"Christ," I say now to myself, lost in the memory.

My mom breaks into my thoughts. "The fact of the matter is, you found that e-mail long before Marco was really ready to discard you. You accelerated the process. And then you kept digging for the truth. Who knows how long he would have devalued you if you hadn't seen that e-mail."

I ponder this for a moment as it sinks in. It wasn't that I magically skipped the devalue phase. It was that I basically forced Marco to discard me before he was ready.

"Mom," I say, "there's something I've blocked for a really long time and just this morning it came back to me. Something that I found at the very beginning, in those days after I found the e-mail."

"There's more? God. OK. What is it?" my mom says, and cups her own coffee mug tightly.

"Do you remember when I looked at the Internet history on our computer? And I found a Google search for the Uber rides to her apartment?"

"Yes . . . ," my mom says nervously.

"Well, there was another Google search that showed up multiple times. I asked him about it and then I think I seriously blocked it from my memory because I just couldn't deal with the real implications of it on top of everything else I was trying to wrap my head around at the time." I take a deep breath. "He Googled 'Does penis enlargement really work?' When I asked him about it, he said he was worried about me being . . . stretched out after having a baby." I look at her with an embarrassed smirk and shudder. "But obviously at this point I know he was researching for Croella."

My mom stares at me. "So while we were all madly trying to help him and figure out what was physically wrong with him. While you stopped producing enough milk for your newborn baby because you were so stressed about the e-mail and his personality change. He was Googling how to make his penis bigger for his twenty-two-year-old girlfriend?"

"Yes," I say.

We stare at each other, and then we both burst out laughing.

"I didn't think anything he did could shock me anymore," my mom says through hysterical laughter.

After a few minutes we quiet down, and I say, "At least we can laugh about it."

"Thank God."

———

I HAVE an appointment with a therapist today. The therapist's office is on the fourth floor of a large brick building in the Old Port. A neighbor recommended this therapist, along with several others, and this is my first consultation, the "getting to know you" visit. It is also my first time ever getting therapy. In fact, I don't even really know what it means, to "get therapy"; I just know that I need to talk to someone who can either validate or veto my amateur Internet diagnosis. I press 4 in the elevator and tug at the sleeve of my green cardigan as the box slowly ascends. The door opens, and I walk down a long hallway and through a doorway to another hallway flanked by small offices with closed doors.

"Hi, Jen?" A very pretty brunette woman pokes her head out the door of an office into the hallway right as I am about to settle into one of the chairs lined up for waiting patients.

"Oh, hi, Lisa?" I say. She is too pretty and too young, I think right away. And in the two small words she has spoken, she gives off an air of self-possession and intelligence. *I used to be like that,* I think to myself as I tug at my sleeve again and follow her into the office.

She tells me to settle in and smiles at me from her cozy chair across the small room. "Is this your first time in therapy?" she asks.

I smile back. "Yes. I'm sorry, I don't really know how it works."

"For this first session, you basically just talk, tell me about your situation, OK?" she says warmly. *Yes, I can do that,* I think, and I begin to talk rapidly in order to bring her up to speed. She listens and nods. Her eyes grow wider as I ramble on, and soon she is leaning forward in her seat. "Wow, this is making me really anxious just hearing about," she says with a laugh halfway through.

"There's so much more," I say, and continue to speak as quickly as I can, determined to finish the whole story in these fifty minutes so that she can fix me. Or at least tell me how to fix myself. I do not mention the word *sociopath.* I do not want to lead her in any way. When I get to the end, I take a deep breath and look up. "So . . . what do you think?" I ask finally.

Lisa folds one long leg under her body. "Some of his behavior sounds to be on the psychopathy spectrum," she says carefully. "I'm going to be honest. In my ten years of practicing, this is one of the most extreme cases of pathology that I've heard."

"Pathology?" I ask. I knew it. He's a sociopath. Now this very smart woman just needs to tell me the exact steps I need to take to heal, and I can start to feel like a person again instead of an empty, aching shell.

"Pathology basically means having destructive, uncontrollable tendencies. I mean, his lying is . . . insane." She laughs. "Or the clinical term would be 'pathological.' He also seems to have a pathological desire to live a double life." She takes a sip of tea from the mug on her side table. "The suicide attempt is interesting because that seems to indicate that he's completely unaware of what he's doing. He's so unwilling to face his lying and pathology that he would rather create this whole 'I lost my mind' charade and take it to the extreme of attempting suicide to validate his version of reality."

"Wait, so . . . a sociopath who doesn't know he's a sociopath? Do some of them know?" I ask in surprise.

"Oh, yes," she says emphatically. "Some sociopathic individuals absolutely know that they suffer from a personality disorder and use it to their advantage. Marco sounds like he lacks empathy and an inner moral compass but that he truly justifies his actions to himself. That's to say, it sounds like he believes his own lies."

I turn this over in my head. It makes me feel better to hear that Marco doesn't seem to even be aware of what he is. That he isn't actually an evil mastermind who looked at me five years ago and thought, *Her. I'm going to destroy her.*

"So, he's acting on pure instinct?" I ask, finishing the thought spinning in my head.

"That's what it sounds like. I also have to warn you, you should prepare yourself to find out about more infidelity that happened over the course of your relationship. It's basically impossible for someone with these types of pathological tendencies to stay faithful to one partner."

My stomach drops. "Oh, no, I know why you would think that, but I really don't think he cheated before this. . . ." I start and then stop. Even to my own ears I sound desperate and pathetic. I can't explain that there is no way he was cheating before November. Because I just know. So, for now, I acquiesce. "I suppose anything is possible."

Leaving Lisa's office, I feel more grounded than I have in months. I am still lost inside the maze of my own mind, but now I have something to hold onto, a cleat in the rock that I can cling to with my fingertips. I climb into the waiting Volvo, and my mom hands me a hungry Louisa.

"How was she?" I ask, brushing back Lulu's hair and undoing my nursing bra.

"She was so good," my mom says. "She's an angel. How was your session? Do you like Lisa?"

"I really do." I recount the session and Lisa's preliminary thoughts.

"Wow, so she really seems to know what she's talking about," my mom says, sipping her to-go latte from the café next door.

"I have a consultation with another therapist set up for tomorrow, so we'll see. But I do get a really good feeling from Lisa."

At the end of my consultation the next day, the very sweet

woman ponders my story and then says, "If you really want to save your marriage, then I think the first thing we need to do is to get Marco to attend a session with you."

I hop into the waiting Volvo again, and this time, I say, "Um. I think I want to keep seeing Lisa."

———

I WAKE up today, and the sun is splashing through my window onto the hardwood floors of my bedroom. I realize it is mid-April. I have been home for more than a month. My parents are in Paris for two weeks, and Stella, Tim, and Henry have moved out of their house and into my parents' house on Haven until my parents get back. "This is gonna be awesome," Tim says in the week leading up to their move-in date. "It's going to be like one big party all the time." No one says the real reason they are moving in is to take care of me. I can now leave the house for a couple of hours at a time, but I am still not functioning normally.

Stella called me last week to say, "So Tim and I were thinking that we could each plan three or four meals. Kind of like a commune! Think about what you would like to cook and let me know so I can do the grocery shopping." When we hung up, I looked at my mom with big eyes. "Stella wants me to cook while you guys are gone," I said anxiously. My mom looked at me with a mixture of horror and incredulity.

"She doesn't understand what it's like over here," she said. "I'll talk to her."

My parents left three days ago, and even though I haven't cooked yet, I feel OK, much better than I thought I would. Today, Stella and I are going to a friend's baby shower. It is my first social gathering since January 20, and as I brush my teeth, cooing to Louisa smiling at me from where she is nestled in a towel on the bathroom floor, I think, *I can do this.*

At the baby shower brunch, I munch on warm croissants and sip pour-over coffee. Louisa shrieks and laughs and tries to claw another baby and everyone *oohs* and *aahs* and says, "She is really something." I glow.

When a friend of my sister's, Kim, sidles up next to me and asks, "How are you doing?" I remember that three years ago, when her son was two, she found out her husband was cheating and using drugs. I don't know the details, but I know that she is raising her son now mostly on her own. The last time I saw her was at my wedding last June.

"You know, today is the first day I woke up and it wasn't the first thing I thought of. I actually feel like I might be able to do this," I say. "It's definitely been really hard, but I think I jumped a major hurdle today because I really feel fine right now." As I am talking I notice that she looks interested and encouraging but perplexed. "Did my sister not tell you?" I ask quickly.

"No," she says with a laugh. "I'm so sorry, I don't know what happened at all."

"Oh, God," I say. "I thought that's why you came over! I found out Marco was having an affair when Louisa was a month old . . . so I'm living with my parents right now and trying to get back on my feet." By now, all eyes are on me. But I feel fine saying this, proud of myself even, that I am able to recite my husband's affair like a recipe from a cookbook. "I think I entered a different phase today. Like maybe I'm over the grief phase? Hopefully anger is next," I say with a laugh, and look around the table. The rest of the women are looking at us, and I notice that the woman who brought the other baby has a tear trickling down her face. I look back to Kim and her face is full of emotion. She's smiling, but her face is twisted up in pain. "No, it's OK, guys," I say. And, in the moment, it is true.

"Do you want to get together sometime? I would really love to talk to you." She gives me her cell, and we make tentative plans to meet up for coffee.

On the drive home, I turn the radio up and hum. It is the first time I have hummed since January 20, and I cry, "Mama's humming again, Lulu! Mama's gonna be OK!" I am excited, even euphoric, about the life that is waiting for me. The person I was always meant to be is now waiting to be discovered; I can feel it.

I nurse Louisa and put her down for a nap in her swing when we get home. I sit down on the couch and a thunder clap erupts in my body, and suddenly I am drowning in sorrow and panic. Four years ago, I was sitting next to Marco in a cozy booth at Doyle's. He stroked my arm and leaned in, whispering in my ear, "Did you know I told you I loved you for the first time last night while you were sleeping?" I looked into his eyes, "I love you, too."

I stand up quickly from the couch and pace around the living room. Tim is working, and Stella is out running errands with Henry. I grab my phone and text my sister, "I'm having a panic attack. I don't understand. I felt so good this morning."

Her response comes quickly. "Oh no, I wanted to talk to you about this before you left the baby shower. I spoke to Kim after you left, and she said 'I know Jenny feels fine today, but it is going to be a really long road. There will be moments when she feels OK and then moments/hours/days when she feels like she is right back to ground zero.' You guys should definitely talk soon. She said even briefly talking to you stirred up a lot of emotions for her."

I take some deep breaths. Reading Stella's text does not take away the tightness in my chest, but it gives me something to hold onto. *It will be OK. It will be OK,* I think on repeat, and circle the living room taking deep breaths. From somewhere far away I hear a booming voice: *"You thought you were fine? Ha!"* I pace some more. There is a buzzing in my head. Through the buzzing, I hear cries coming from upstairs. I move on autopilot up the stairs and scoop a whimpering Louisa from her swing. I tell her everything is going to be OK and kiss her hair over and over. I'm not going to make it. I'm not going to make it through this. My jaw won't unclench, and my eyes are wide and burning. I hear a text come in. It's Stella. "I'm almost back. Do you want to go for a walk?"

"Yes," I respond to my sister. I breathe in and open and close my mouth to relax my jaw.

Stella and I stroll to the beach that is a fifteen-minute walk away.

"I felt fine this morning. I felt like I understood things. Like I understood basically what happened. Like, it happens. Men cheat. Marco had really bad timing. But then when I really think about it, about him and about us and how we were and our memories and . . ."

"I know," Stella cuts in gently. "Jenny, this wasn't a normal 'married dude who cheated' situation. You can't think of it like that. We all loved Marco, and he turned out to be a completely different person than we thought. But the really crazy part to me is the lying and continuing to try to play both sides as long as he did. I don't understand what he was thinking. Did he think he was going to get away with it?"

Her simple question jolts me for a second. "Yes," is on the tip of my tongue, but it doesn't feel right. Did he actually *want* to get away with it? I ask myself.

"I think," I say, shaping my thoughts into words, "I think he wanted to get caught. I don't think he wanted to fix things. I think he wanted me to be forced to leave."

My sister sighs. "He's a coward."

We turn right onto Willow Street, which leads to a long, sandy beach and expanse of brilliant ocean. Henry hops out of his stroller and runs on his miniature legs to the playground at the edge of the beach. I unstrap Lulu's seat belt and lift her into my lap, sitting in the shade on the small wooden boardwalk beside the playground. I look around at the kids playing and laughing. Adults yelling and forcefully applying suntan lotion to flailing limbs.

Oh no, I think. I can feel it coming, the panic attack. There is black ink streaming out of the pit in my stomach, and soon it will cover all of my insides. I squint my eyes and try to focus on Lulu's soft hair and the sand tickling my toes. The noises around me rise to a fevered pitch and then jumble together to form a high-pitched buzzing. "Shut up," I want to scream at the mom yelling to her three-year-old to let his friend have a turn and the two ladies carrying on a casual conversation to my right. "How can you be so normal? How can you be talking about grocery shopping when my whole world has crashed down and I am drowning in my own body?"

"I have to go," I call to Stella. "I don't feel well." I wave to her worried face and turn around quickly. She cannot leave Henry and she cannot pick him up because she is nine months pregnant, and I am grateful because I am not going to make it if she comes over here. I drop Lulu into her stroller, fasten her seat belt, and I am off the boardwalk, off the beach, and onto the street before my face crumples, and I start to cry.

I just don't understand how this happened. How does Marco have a girlfriend and I am with our three-month-old baby alone in Maine? How did he change into a completely different person overnight? How is he still doing it? How has he not apologized? Suddenly, I realize that I am actually still waiting for a genuine, heartfelt apology. *"I'm so sorry that I started fucking someone else right when you gave birth and betrayed you and lied to you and treated you like my enemy and destroyed you so completely that there is nothing left."* Is that what I expect?

He is never going to feel remorse or guilt. He still thinks he is the victim in this situation.

I remember all the research I have done on psychopathy. That the psychopath's personality was never real, that the psychopath never felt love or genuine intimacy. The psychopath sees all other people as mere objects, not human beings. Objects that immediately lose their value if they are no longer feeding the psychopath's ego. *I was a toaster,* I remind myself. A toaster that no longer worked and therefore no longer had any use to Marco. Me wanting Marco to fall on his knees and express remorse for what he has done is like a broken toaster demanding a heartfelt apology as it is carted away to the dump. *"You used me up and then threw me away like I was nothing. How could you just replace me right away? How could you?"* I imagine its whinnying, metallic cries.

By the time I am pushing Louisa up the rocky driveway, I am

breathing normally. I play with Lulu and nurse her and tell her that eventually, soon, I will be better. I look at the clock and somehow it is 5:00 P.M. I sigh with relief and start Lulu's tubby. As I nurse her, her eyes flicker shut, and I think, *I made it. I am going to make it.*

BEFORE

LOUISA was almost two weeks old, and the two of us had just spent more than a week in Maine with my parents. Those ten days were the height of Louisa's colic, and she vacillated between soft fussing and enraged screaming the entire time. My parents and I took turns walking her around and around and around the kitchen, bouncing and shushing, pausing near the refrigerator in the hopes that the white noise would finally lull her to sleep. Much of the time I was not soothing Louisa, I spent on my phone, Googling "newborn screams nonstop" and texting Marco things like "I think we made a terrible mistake" and "I can't do this." I told my parents I shouldn't have come to Maine.

"I need to be near Marco," I said through tears on the third day home. "I can't do this."

"Jen, I know it's so, so hard, but he wouldn't even be able to help you right now. He said he would barely be home while his boss is on vacation."

I knew that if I was in New York, I would be alone in the apartment with Louisa most of the time and her screaming wouldn't magically stop, but I felt with every cell of my body that if I could just be near Marco, I would be less anxious. Those ten days seemed like an eternity. When I finally got back to New York, after a six-hour drive—throughout which Louisa slept almost the entire way, thank God—I collapsed into Marco's arms and let out all the air in my lungs from the past ten days.

"My babies," he said, breathing me in, kissing my forehead and lips, and then kneeling down to the car seat and kissing a sleeping, angelic Louisa, and I thought, *Of course she decides to sleep for six hours straight today.*

Marco was late for work and rushing out the door, but just being with him for a few moments made the past couple of weeks suddenly seem less horrible. I watched him scramble around, buttoning up his shirt and tightening his belt, and I thought, *It will be OK. We can get through this together.* Before he left, he paused in front of the door and said, "Oh crap, babe, I kinda sorta broke the bed a couple nights ago."

"What do you mean?" I asked him, exasperated. "Where am I going to sleep tonight?"

"It will hold for a while, but one of the legs of the bed frame snapped so the bed kind of slopes to one side. I sat on the end of the bed really hard a few nights ago," he said sheepishly.

"Jesus, fatso!" I said.

"Hey! I just have a large badonkadonk," he said, slipping on his tie and grabbing his suit jacket. "Oh, and I also took all the bedsheets to the laundromat. I wanted to make the bed with new sheets before you got home, but I've just been running around and now I have to leave. . . ."

"Marco. Seriously? I have to make the bed after a six-hour drive? You do know I just gave birth, right?"

"Baby, I'm sorry, I really didn't have time. But I love you so much? And you're the most amazing wife ever in the world?"

"You're really, really lucky that I've missed you so much for the past ten days," I said as he leaned in to kiss me one more time from the doorway.

"I missed you, too. I missed you guys so much, you have no idea."

After Marco left for work, I climbed up on a kitchen chair, straining to reach bedsheets and a fresh duvet cover from the top of the closet. The area in between my legs was still sore and swollen from the second-degree tear I got pushing out Louisa, and I was lightheaded from the six-hour drive and the overload of hormones still coursing through my body. It took me forty minutes to make the bed and fit the comforter into the duvet cover. I cried when I finally finished and laid down. The bed sank so far to one side that I almost rolled off. My dad ended up coming over that night and wedging a suitcase under the frame to temporarily keep the bed level. After he left, I tiptoed back into the bedroom and laid down silently, listening for Louisa's soft snores from her crib at the foot of the bed. I knew she would be up to nurse in a couple of hours, and I shut my eyes tightly, willing myself to sleep. My eyes flicked open to a text message from Marco lighting up my phone: "I'm so happy you guys are home."

I closed my eyes again and felt my body relax. Louisa's snores lulled me to sleep.

AFTER

MY parents arrived home from Paris yesterday. Today my mom had the idea to check our Seamless, GrubHub, and iTunes accounts the Sunday that Marco had off while Louisa and I were in Maine.

"I bet you anything he ordered a bunch of food and movies and she was there the entire day," my mom says. "And that's when they broke the bed."

We are trying to piece together exactly what happened during the months of December and January. I have been in the dark for so long, and there have been so many lies, that I am digging and digging for whatever truth I can find through my amateur detective work. Marco still messages me on a regular basis that "there was never any physical relationship with that person." If Marco will never, ever own up, then I want just one concrete piece of evidence so that there is no longer even the tiniest bit of me that wonders.

"There's a ton of Seamless and GrubHub orders, but they're

not just on his day off. Look, we left for Maine on January first, right? That was a Thursday. He was working nonstop, the entire time we were gone. But look at Friday and Saturday nights. And then again the next week. He ordered food to our apartment a bunch of nights around eight P.M. That doesn't make any sense. He was working those nights. He was working the entire time we were in Maine," I say again. My mind bangs together these two contrasting pieces of information and then fizzles. I can't make sense of the online food orders. "Maybe he went into work really, really late?" Even to my own ears the words sound hollow and false.

My mom puts on her reading glasses and peers at my phone.

"Jen," she says matter-of-factly, "he wasn't working while we were in Maine. That's why the phone calls started on January eleventh. Marco and Viktorija were together the entire time we were in Maine right after Louisa was born."

I have the familiar feeling of my brain being covered in sludge as I try to make an argument for why this can't be true. The thought passes through my head quickly, *But he was furious he didn't get any days off when Louisa was born. There's no way he took time off while we were in Maine,* but it evaporates before it makes its way to my mouth. And then my mom says what I've already pieced together somewhere deep in the cavernous walls of my foggy brain.

"He took paternity days while you and Lulu were in Maine. He spent them with Croella at your apartment."

———

WHILE Louisa naps, I go to the websites about sociopaths again. I click on a sublink that reads "Sociopaths: A Lack of Conscience." I read that sociopaths have absolutely no conscience.

Whenever they seemingly do something that falls in line with so-
cietal standards of "good" or "moral" it is only because it benefits
them in some way. While they are smart enough to understand
that society deems certain things (cheating, lying, murder, rape)
as "bad," they do not actually *feel* that there is anything wrong
with these things. Most sociopaths don't murder or rape because
they understand that there would be very large, and bothersome,
consequences if they got caught, not because their conscience or
inner moral compass is conflicted about such acts. In fact, they
have no inner moral compass. The only voice that directs their
actions is the voice that says, "This feeds my ego and feels good,"
or "This is advantageous to me." The concept of right and wrong
is beneath them. They believe they are superior to most people,
and so the rules that apply to everyone else do not apply to them.
For every time my brain screams, *You will never understand. Stop
trying,* another voice booms, *You must make sense of what happened
to you.*

It is not the cheating that fills my mind almost every waking
minute now; it is the abrupt change in personality from adoring
husband to heartless stranger. I have always, on some level, understood relationships that crumble and end in cheating and bitter-
ness. "To be honest, I saw that coming," I would say to my friends
when the news hit about another long-term couple going through
a horrific breakup. Or, "I'm not super surprised," I told my mom,
about the neighbors embattled in a bitter divorce, who had had a
habit of getting overly tipsy and slamming each other with passive-
aggressive one-liners at the neighborhood holiday parties. But my
marriage? My husband? My Marco?

I look back at the sublink titles. "Cognitive Dissonance: When

Your Heart and Brain Can't Get on the Same Page." I click. Anyone involved in a relationship with a psychopath goes through a long period of something called cognitive dissonance. It is a period of time during which you are trying to merge two realities: that the person you thought was your best friend and the love of your life is actually nothing but an illusion; his sole objective was to build you up so that he could destroy you in the worst way possible. Even a "low-functioning" sociopath like Marco, who may not be aware of his own personality disorder, makes his way through life with the instinctive mission to conquer and destroy. Many targets cling to denial for months as they stubbornly refuse to believe that the person they were madly in love with a few months earlier, the person who seemingly worshipped them, is now cold and dismissive. Even while encountering more and more lies and evidence of infidelity, they try to reclaim and relive the blissful period they had at the beginning of the relationship. An internal battle wages between the heart and brain as contradictory realities clash against one another. I was idealized for five years. My reality was solid for five years and then torn to shreds overnight.

"Well, fuck, no wonder," I mutter to myself as I read that cognitive dissonance often presents itself in panic attacks as your mind alternates between trying to digest and suppress these conflicting realities. Under the thread about cognitive dissonance, I see a thread titled, "Gaslighting—One of the P's Favorite Tools."

"What the hell is gaslighting?" I ask, clicking on the link. Gaslighting is a psychological tool that psychopaths use to mess with their victims' hold on reality during the devalue phase. It's a form of mental manipulation that eventually causes the target to question her own sanity and to mistrust her perception of reality.

The most common example is a P denying something he said or did. The P is so adamant and incredulous in his denial that his partner second-guesses herself and then finally decides that she must be confused, misremembering, going insane. I think back to the day Marco tagged and then untagged me in the sunglasses picture. How easily I decided to let it go; how easily I let myself be convinced that I was probably confused—maybe Marco never tagged the picture, maybe I was going insane from sleep deprivation. And then of course there is the outright denial, first of any kind of relationship, then of a physical relationship with Croella, for months. Even now, as I find myself playing detective, doubting that I'll ever know the truth is still driving me slightly crazy.

"Christ almighty, does he have a fucking sociopath handbook?" I ask out loud to my computer. Before I realize what I'm doing, I have Googled the name of the apartment broker. I find his work e-mail. I type furiously and then hit send. He will never respond. There is no way he will ever respond.

Twenty minutes later my phone rings. I look down at the area code, and I know it is the broker. Holy fuck. I clumsily answer my phone.

"Hello?" I say through a short spurt of breath.

"Jen?" His voice sounds far away and mumbled. "I got your e-mail. Usually I wouldn't stick my nose in something like this, but I felt considering the circumstances, I had to call you."

I can barely hear him. I stick my finger in my other ear and close my eyes.

"I showed your husband and a blonde, Eastern European girl two apartments in Manhattan." His voice comes through crystal clear, and I realize he has taken me off speakerphone at the same time that I realize what he has just said. "Sometime in early January. They were holding hands and kissing. There was another listing agent there who can verify. I'm . . ." He clears his throat awkwardly. "I'm very sorry to tell you this."

"Thank you," I say gratefully. "Thank you so much."

I hang up and run downstairs and tell my mom. She hugs me tightly. I'm crying and laughing incredulously.

"Finally, Jenny," she says. "We finally know."

———

"YOU need to try to keep the thirty-thousand-foot view," my mom tells me as I peer down at Cruella's Instagram profile for the thirtieth time today. "Don't get lost down in all the details. Think about the big picture. Think about what he's already done. Seeing new pictures isn't going to change the fundamental horrific things he's already done."

I know she's right. Nothing I could find out at this point could be worse. And really, why would it matter anyway? So I try to take my mom's advice and look down from above the clouds, but I find myself falling to the ground a hundred times a day. Is he with her now? I wonder. Does he call her "babe" or "baby"? Is he the one who took her new profile picture at Central Park? I know these things don't matter. They don't change the outcome of what has already happened. I am a single mom living with my parents, and my life has been put in a snow globe and shaken so hard that the glass has cracked. Yet, I think about him constantly. I am obsessed with finding more and more proof that they are in some kind of sick relationship. Of course I know that they have been "together" for months, but Marco texts dozens of times a day adamantly denying that he is still involved with Croella. He says he is working on his "recovery" and finding "old Marco." He tells me he's made progress as to why he did what he did. (But *what* did you do, Marco? Can you actually say it yet?) He tells me that he wants his wife back; he wants his life back and everything that he had. When I ask him to remove her as a Facebook friend and unfollow her on Instagram, out of respect for me and Louisa, he becomes angry and aggressive or is completely silent. I know it is immature and pointless to make these requests. If he had any respect for me and Louisa he wouldn't have broken our bed with another woman. But I need to call his bluff. I want him to know that I am no longer falling for his act. It is a silly game to play considering the gravity of what he has done. I know that the very fact that I am playing means that he is still winning. But I don't know how to let him go completely. This fucked-up thing is better than nothing. The dynamic that we used to have has been so completely destroyed that I am left clinging to texts that switch between being outright cruel and sappy and lovey. Sometimes they come in literally one right after another. I went from trusting and loving this person, from feeling adored and protected, to licking bitter morsels that he is throwing at me off the ground whenever he senses that I am starting to break free. Now I understand why sociopaths are dubbed "human heroin." I have been shooting pure, unadulterated psychopathic love into my bloodstream for five years. I am coming down from a drug I didn't even know I was on, and the withdrawal has knocked me on my fucking ass.

———

"I DON'T know if you'll be required to report me to the authorities if I tell you this," I say to Lisa with a nervous laugh at our next session, "but I still know Marco's social media passwords because he's an idiot. I check his profiles quite a bit. I know I shouldn't," I say quickly, "but it's become kind of an OCD thing."

Lisa laughs. "First of all, the only time I am required to report you to the authorities is if you make a statement that I feel indicates that you are seriously contemplating hurting yourself or someone else. You're still married to Marco, correct?" she asks.

I nod. "Yes."

"Then I'm pretty sure it's not a crime. Let me ask you something, though. When you log in, do you get kind of a rush of nervous adrenaline followed by almost like a comedown?"

"Yes," I say, nodding emphatically. "Yes, that's exactly what it feels like."

"OK, so that sounds like obsessive-compulsive behavior, and it's pretty common when wading through the aftermath of a trauma. It's a coping mechanism. In fact, I would even say it's a necessary stage. The thing we need to be careful of, though, is that eventually you replace that obsessive-compulsive behavior with something healthier. There's a fine line between this being a phase of your recovery and you becoming addicted to this 'keeping tabs' type of behavior. For now, though, we don't need to worry about that. You're still early on in beginning to process this trauma."

"OK, that's really good to know." I immediately feel better.

"But let me ask you something else. What is it you're looking for exactly when you check Marco's profile? You already have a ton of proof of his affair."

"Good question." I sit back against the couch and ponder her question for a moment. "You know, I think there's still a large part of my brain that wants to actually see an interaction between the two of them, because he's still denying that it's a relationship. He's basically at this point like a kid caught with his hand *in* the cookie jar, saying, 'Huh? I'm not taking a cookie, I swear.' Even though the broker called me, and I know he had and is almost certainly still having this affair, it's like the mere fact that he won't actually own up to it is driving me crazy. Which is probably half the fun for him in continuing to deny it," I say.

"No, that makes sense," Lisa says. "Most men who have affairs either end the affair, or, if they get caught but continue it, they are forced to admit its existence. Marco is seemingly continuing it but still not owning up. He seems adamant in directing attention toward his so-called mental breakdown. So it's like this elephant in the room. You know the affair happened and is still happening, but he's acting like it's all in your imagination. Or that you don't have a right to focus on it because everyone should be focusing on his mental health."

"Right, exactly. If I can just see some actual physical evidence, like a picture or a message between the two of them . . ." My voice trails off. "I don't know. I don't even know how that would make me feel," I admit.

"Right, well, that's why I asked in the first place. Because I really do think that you should be heading toward absolutely no contact with Marco. Any contact with him has a negative effect on you and messes with your perception of reality and what you know to be true. He's living in Crazy Land, and I don't want you to get dragged there, too."

I leave Lisa's office determined to break contact with Marco once and for all. For two weeks, I try not to respond to his texts—and for two weeks, I fail. They come in every day, dozens of them, and ping-pong between hurtful and cruel and intense love bombing. I am so exhausted that finally, I make a firm decision. I will have no contact with Marco for one week. If I make it through the next week, then I'll take it from there. One week. I can do this. I send Marco a one-line text: "I'm not going to talk to you for a while." His response comes in a few minutes later: "Whatever, Jen."

The first twenty-four hours of no contact I almost don't make it. I didn't realize that the dosing out of negative and positive communication with him was giving me just enough of a high to make it through the day. I have been withdrawing slowly for months now, but having no contact makes me feel like I have gone cold turkey. I feel physically ill; I break into cold sweats. I shake. I have to retreat to my bedroom several times to lay down and cry. The next twenty-four hours are just as bad. I stare at my phone. I take deep breaths. I nurse Louisa as I reread days' worth of texts from Marco. I look at pictures from our wedding, our honeymoon, my pregnancy. I kiss Louisa's head over and over, but she is blurry, always blurry. I look at Louisa and I try to see her, to really see her, but instead I see everything that we have lost. I take walks with my mom. I don't know how to tell her that I am withdrawing from a potent drug, so I say numbly, "This is really hard." On the third day, on my way to see Lisa, I receive a text from Marco. My adrenaline surges, my eyes focus. "Jennifer, please send me pictures of Louisa. I don't want to have to take you to court but I will. Thank you." I bite my nails. I feel sick. I feel guilty. I ask Lisa what to do.

"You don't owe him a goddamned thing," she says immediately. "If you really feel that guilty, send a couple pictures to his parents. If he wants to get a divorce, then fine, let him get a divorce. Let him take you to court." Her eyes flash. She is angrier than I am.

"I wish I could be angry. Instead of sad and guilty and heart-broken," I say.

"It will come," Lisa says. "Trust me."

———

THE same night, I get another text from Marco. My hands shake as I unlock my home screen. I am equal parts fearful and ea-ger, like a crack addict picking up a pipe from the sidewalk and sniffing the tip. I brace myself for anger, or worse, something curt and indifferent. Instead, I see a picture of his left hand. His wedding band shines front and center. Underneath the picture is a long para-graph: "I have been doing a lot of thinking lately. I want you to know that I am slowly finding the man that you fell in love with once. I also want you to know that I am never, ever taking off my wedding band. I broke one promise to you and this is a promise that I will not break. I will carry it with me wherever I go. I hope you are doing better than me. Don't reply. I just wanted you to know." I read the message five times and then copy and paste the text to Nat.

"Wow, this must mean that Croella broke up with him, huh?" Nat replies right away.

I ponder her assumption. Everything I have read about psy-chopaths so far would indicate that Marco love bombing me in no way means that he has stopped pursuing his other targets. My fin-gers itch to reply, to connect again. Instead, I research more about psychopathy. I read more about the tactics that psychopaths use during the initial idealize phase, and, to a lesser extent, when they are trying to reel you back in after a discard. I come across an article that discusses at length a tactic called "the pity play." Because psychopaths tend to target individuals who are especially empathetic and trusting, the best way to win a target is to appeal to her decency. The psychopath will weave an elaborate sob story, pouring his heart out to his target and making her feel not only sympathetic to the psychopath's "bad luck" but also extremely flattered that the psychopath has chosen *her* to divulge his deepest secrets to. I think about all those nights spent in dark, musty bars. Marco lowering his eyes and revealing his broken family and living in the shadows illegally for all those years. Me, reaching across the table and touching his arm, so moved at his vulnerability, his raw emotions.

I text Nat about my new research and the discovery of the pity play.

Does Marco actually fit the sociopathic profile to a T, or am I seeing what I want to see? Picking and choosing the traits that match up and ignoring the loose ends. My heart seizes as I remember our day-to-day life together. Marco cooking his famous pork chops in our hot and sticky apartment in August. Placing the plates down on the table with a flourish as I mixed cranberry juice and seltzer into big glasses full of ice. Sipping coffee from oversize mugs on a Sunday morning. Jogging to Long Island City and then pressing our sweaty bodies together in a celebratory hug when we reached the boardwalk. No, Marco can't be a psychopath. He is a sick man, and he had a mental breakdown. My mind spins in circles as I drift to sleep and try to answer the question that keeps popping up: If he was truly sick, then why aren't we together right now?

Over the next several days, Marco's love bombing gets more

and more desperate. When he texts me, my parents, and Nat that he has found a job in Maine and is looking for apartments in Portland, I Google "ignoring a sociopath." Interesting. One article says to think of a sociopath as a three-year-old adult, since, developmentally, that is about right (toddlers have not yet developed self-control or empathy, so physiologically their brains are similar to the psychopathic adult). When you ignore a three-year-old, or let's say, take away his favorite toy, what happens? Judging from my own extremely well-behaved nephew, there would be a short period of whining followed by an all-out temper tantrum. The same can be said for an adult sociopath. I realize that what I am witnessing is not Marco regaining his true feelings or recovering his love for me and Louisa; he is having an adult temper tantrum. I close the computer and try to ignore the tiny voice that whispers, "But maybe, just maybe he really is realizing what he lost. . . ."

It has been a week now of not responding to Marco. I made it. I am still shaky, but I feel OK. Marco's love bombing has continued, with intermittent threats of taking me to court, and I have not responded. I celebrate by asking my sister and Tim to babysit while I go to therapy and then get a pedicure. I have had a pedicure maybe four times in my life, but right now, luxuriating in the vibrating leather salon chair and soaking my feet in warm soapy water, I can't imagine anything better in the world. While the chair rumbles against my neck, I think about Lisa's response to Marco's recent texts. I read her a particularly epic text that somehow combined love bombing, threatening court, and demanding a response to whether I wanted him to move to Maine all in one paragraph.

"Wow. Well, first of all, that is so textbook sociopathic."

"What do you mean? How so?" I asked.

"Him going on and on about how he's made a ton of progress in his 'recovery' and that he's looking for a job and apartments in Maine? That is classic sociopath. To say he's jumped ahead to 'recovery' before he's actually done any work. It would take him years, and I mean *years*, of serious, hard work to even have a chance at recovery. He would have to *learn* empathy and build a conscience. Even then, he wouldn't actually *feel* empathy. To be honest, psychopathy isn't actually curable. There's no medication for it, and therapy doesn't work. I try to keep the belief that with years and years of doing the really hard, deep work, a sociopath could maybe at least lessen, or become more aware of, their sociopathic attributes. But him saying he's basically recovered is ridiculous."

The rest of the day unfolds without incident, but as I am nursing Louisa to sleep, my heart starts to throb, and I break into a cold sweat. *Oh no,* I think. *No, stay strong.* I place Louisa in her crib and ignore the tightness in my chest. I pace around the kitchen. I pour myself a glass of rosé. I feel it coming. I run to my bedroom and throw myself on the bed. I try to muffle the sounds of my cries with a pillow. I can't breathe. I am going to suffocate. "Please call me, it's an emergency," I text to Marco. Five minutes later, my phone rings.

"What's wrong?" His voice fills my ear. It is the warm, concerned, sweet voice of my old husband. This was a bad idea.

"I'm just not doing well," I say. "I shouldn't have asked you to call."

"Are you OK?" he asks. I can't say anything. "Gin? I promise everything is going to be OK. I don't know why this happened. I don't know how I hurt the person that I love most in the world. But I promise you"—his tone oozes with earnestness—"I will make sure everything is OK." I want to bury myself in his warm, sweet voice.

"I have to go. I shouldn't have asked you to call," I say again numbly. I hang up and call Nat. I tell her about my panic attack.

"Have you had lots of caffeine today? Or any alcohol?" she asks.

I think about the two cups of coffee this morning and the wine after my pedicure. "Yes. Does that cause anxiety?"

"It definitely contributes. Drink a glass of water."

Before we hang up, she says, "At least it sounds like he is starting to realize what a shithead he is and how horrible and stupid he's been."

I walk downstairs and pour myself a glass of water. I focus on the cool liquid gliding down my throat. There is a nagging in my stomach. I grab my phone and bring up Gmail. My fingers tremble as I type in Marco's e-mail and then his usual password. This isn't going to work. He had to have changed his password. "Oh my God," I mutter as the screen redirects me to Marco's in-box. The first e-mail I see is an OpenTable reservation reminder. For tonight. I open the e-mail. Mercer Kitchen. The reservation is for 8:30 P.M. I glance at the clock. It is 9:30 P.M. He must have been out to dinner when he called me. Before my brain fully registers what this means, I am bringing up Croella's Instagram profile. The last picture uploaded is of a large bouquet of white flowers. "Birthday flowers" is the caption, with an emoticon of a monkey hiding his face.

My stomach plummets and my mind races back to three years ago, my twenty-eighth birthday . . . "Welcome to Mercer Kitchen."

"That fucker," I say out loud. My birthday restaurant. He

took her to *our* restaurant. For her twenty-third birthday. A stran-gled sound bubbles out of my throat. I bring up the forum I have found for people recovering from psychopathic relationships and click on the thread that caught my eye a few days ago. It is titled "Why do P's lack imagination?" I read message after message of people recounting similar incidents. "He took the other woman to the same place we went for our honeymoon. How can he be so aw-ful?" one woman writes. I scan the thread and finally see that a moderator has chimed in near the end, providing an explanation: "It's not that P's are trying to be intentionally cruel, though they could care less about that since they have no conscience. Rather, since P's lack an identity, they spend their lives collecting data and analyzing situations. They merely see that something 'works' and so store it away for future use on another target."

I tiptoe upstairs and into the bathroom. I sit on the toilet and text Nat that Marco is currently with Croella at the restaurant he took me to three years ago for my birthday.

"Are you FUCKING kidding me?" she replies.

"I don't know whether to laugh or cry," I write back.

"Well, I actually started laughing when I first read your text and now I'm crying for you because . . . WTF."

When I read Nat's text, I start laughing, too. My laughter becomes hysterical and soon I am doubled over, tears running down my face. Marco's face pops into my head. The face that smiled at me in wonder as we danced to "Happy" with Seb. I chant "he's dead" through my hysteria, and now my head is in between my knees and snot and tears run together. I wipe my face with toilet paper, stand up, and look in the mirror. "He's dead," I say one more time before splashing cold water into my eyes.

———

AS much as I try to direct my thoughts away from Marco and Croella, I find myself getting stuck on how Marco convinced her to fall for him. I don't understand what he could have said. I try to think about this as objectively as possible. I force myself to go back to the early days of our relationship. He told me that he had been miserable for years and that I was an "angel" sent down from heaven. Could he have told her the same thing? That he was in a loveless, unhappy marriage? But he plastered Facebook and Instagram with the two of us. A couple of months before Louisa's birth he posted a picture of the two of us with the caption "My love. My life." How could he have said he was unhappy? How could she have believed him?

"He couldn't have said the same things," I say to my mom that afternoon as we stroll with Louisa, repeating what has been circulating in my head for months. "He told me that he had been miserable for years, and it lined up with what Nat and his family said later. And they had no pictures together for the past three years. Zero. I know social media is a strange thing to consider, but when Marco and Viktorija became Facebook friends in November his profile picture was from our maternity photo shoot. And Tania and him weren't married and expecting a baby. It was a completely different situation." I think about if, five years ago, I had known that Marco and Tania were married and that she was eight months pregnant, could he have somehow still convinced me? My stomach turns at the thought.

"You're right, it was a very different situation. But it might not have taken much convincing. Maybe he said it was all an act, that he was pretending to be the adoring husband because he wanted his green card. Maybe he really said he was having a mental breakdown. Most likely, we'll never understand."

Nevertheless, I find myself morbidly fixated on trying to understand.

"But why? Why did she want to be with a man who would do that to his wife and baby?" I find myself asking my best friends. Their responses range from "She's one in a million. There are not many women who could be convinced, no matter what the guy said, to do what she did," to "Marco sniffs out insecurities like a bloodhound. I'm sure all he had to do was tell her she was special and she was flat on her back." I ask Lisa at our next session, and she says, "There are millions of things he could have said. My guess is that he told her your pregnancy was unplanned and he felt trapped."

"But, by the time they met, he had already posted dozens of pictures of me pregnant with cute little captions and statuses about the baby and how excited he was. I mean, I know he could have said he was lying on social media for whatever reason, but that seems a little thin, don't you think?"

Lisa is quiet for a minute. "You may never be able to figure out exactly what he said. It could have been as simple as 'I thought I was happy until I met you.' He targeted her because she's extremely insecure, and he figured out how to give her whatever validation she needed. For someone who has been looking to be validated her entire life, do you know how powerful it would be to hear 'I'm giving up everything for you'?" I think back to the person I was when I met Marco. I was desperate for external validation. I needed someone to tell me I was special so that I could believe it myself. I decided that Marco was my missing piece and because of his love, I would finally be whole. I wanted so badly to feel the "magic" of love, to be adored, to find my fairy-tale ending, to be complete. Even when I found out that Tania was still in the picture, I convinced myself that Marco and I were soul mates, that we were destined to be together, and that Tania was just an obstacle we had to overcome. Rather than seeing Marco's bad behavior as a major character flaw, I justified Marco's cheating and lying as a means to an end—the "end" being us together forever, happily ever after.

Lisa continues. "And honestly, do you really think that a mature woman who had an ounce of self-respect would want to be involved with a married man whose wife is nine months pregnant? There are probably a few different things going on that created the perfect storm."

Finally, I ask Nat, and she is the first person who laughs. "Oh, you're so cute. There are literally hundreds of girls like her in New York. I guarantee you it took absolutely zero convincing. She just didn't care. I know you grew up in a place where you didn't run into these kinds of people, but I'm telling you there are many, many people with extremely loose morals and absolutely zero boundaries. You want to psychoanalyze it, but the answer is pretty straightforward: She didn't give a fuck."

"Really? You really think there are other people who would do what she did?"

She laughs again. "Hundreds. Thousands. Do you know how many people, especially in New York, have the attitude 'fuck everyone else'? Have you seen Croella's Instagram? She's constantly posting either selfies or quotes that say things like, 'If you don't like my attitude, fuck off.' I mean, it might be hard to accept, but there are a lot of bad people in the world. Or at least people who do bad things."

I try to absorb this perspective. I know I am fixated on understanding Croella's motivations and frame of mind because I can't
face trying to dissect the poisonous tangles inside Marco's head.
What he did is a dark, gaping black hole. I know that if I jump in,
I will not find meaning, a light bulb will not go off and illuminate
the cavernous walls; rather, I will get sucked into the darkness and
never be able to find my way out. And then a voice in my head says
very clearly, "She could have been anyone." The obviousness and
the truth of this statement jolts me. If it wasn't her, it would have
been someone else. Marco hunted for someone willing to feed his
ego, but it didn't actually matter to him who it was. I fall asleep not
thinking, *How did you do it, Marco?* but *How did you trick me for five
years?*

BEFORE

"OH my God, today is January twentieth, Seb's birthday!" I said to Marco, placing Louisa into the cloth newborn carrier and wrapping it securely around my waist.

"I know, I know, things have been so crazy with work and the baby that I completely dropped the ball on his birthday." Marco rubbed his eyes and took a gulp of coffee. We'd been up off and on all night with Lulu. It was 6:45 A.M., but the hours blurred together now and it felt like the middle of the day. Marco poured coffee into a second mug and set it down on the coffee table. "Do you think you can pick him up a present today, and I'll try to plan a party with Nat for some time next week?"

"Of course. I'll go with my parents. I know how much you've been working. You're pushing yourself too hard, babe." I took a swig of coffee and then set it back down and began power walking up and down the hallway. "She's gotta be tired, right? I mean, she didn't sleep at all last night."

"I don't know." Marco plopped down on the couch. "I guess we have a nocturnal baby."

"Actually, that's true of all newborns," I called from the end of the hallway. "The sleep book says that babies can't distinguish between day and night until they're a few weeks old."

"Great," Marco said.

"Hey, do you know what would be nice?" I said excitedly. "If we all surprised Seb when he gets off the bus this afternoon—with some cupcakes and balloons? What do you think?"

"I can't today," Marco moaned as he stretched his legs onto the coffee table. "I have to go into work early."

"Oh, really? Shoot. OK, well, I'll go with Lulu and my parents. His birthday needs to be celebrated in some way today, don't you think?"

"It would be great if you and your parents could do something for him. I wish I could go with you guys. I hate my job."

"It's not really right for your boss to be making you work all these extra hours. Especially right now. Having you around is the only thing that is keeping me sane. Can you talk to him about cutting you some slack?" I asked, bobbing up and down in front of the couch. "I think she's asleep, thank Jesus."

"He's crazy, babe," Marco said with a groan. "He doesn't care that we just had a baby. And he doesn't care that I haven't seen Seb in two months. The restaurant didn't do as well as he projected during the holidays and he's freaking out now. He wants me there every day at one P.M. instead of three P.M. so we can go over numbers and talk strategy going forward. And he wants me to be the last one out every night now, too. So I won't be getting home til four A.M. at the earliest for the next few weeks."

"Marco, that's really insane," I said. "The nights are really hard and I need—"

"Babe, trust me, the one thing in the world I want to do is stay home with you and the baby. I've barely even spent any time with her since she was born. It's driving me crazy. I promise I'll talk to my boss in a few weeks. I'm going to ask for a week off so I can be home full-time with you guys."

"OK, that would be so great." I took another deep breath and rubbed my eyes. "I'm so exhausted. I honestly don't know what I would do without you."

"Let's go get some breakfast while the baby is sleeping," Marco said, getting up from the couch. He looked at me closely. "Do you want me to take her while you brush your hair?"

"Oh." I looked in the mirror on the opposite wall. My hair was sticking out in ten different directions. "I guess I haven't really brushed my hair in a couple days."

"Here." He held out his arms. I undid the baby carrier straps from my waist and carefully handed Louisa to Marco. I started to walk toward the bedroom and then paused. "I really love you, Marco. I just didn't expect this to be so hard—"

"Baby." He cut me off. "I promise things will get a lot easier soon. We just have to ride this out."

"Right, OK," I said, too tired to argue. "Things have to get easier soon, right? They have to."

AFTER

I LISTEN to the words that I'm hearing on the other end of the phone, but my mind is a blank. How do I process this information that I'm receiving? How is it possible that I can hear something at this point that shocks me, that turns my stomach, that turns my mind into mush? Let's back up. A friend who used to frequent the Thirsty Owl popped up today in a Facebook message, saying she'd been thinking about me and asked how I was doing. I told her to call me and now I am on the phone with her, telling her the story that I have now filed down to a few key details: found e-mail, emotional affair, suicide attempt, broker call, broken bed. She *oob*s and *aab*s and gasps in all the right places. When I think the conversation is over, her tone changes. "Jen," she says, "I have to tell you something. I've been going over and over in my head whether or not to tell you, but I feel you have a right to know and you seem to be in an OK place to hear this now." I am thinking, *Hear what?!*

What more could there possibly be to hear? "Look, the reason Steve and Michelle always hated Marco so much? They caught him having sex in the Thirsty Owl when you guys first opened ... on three separate occasions with three different women. And I guess his friend Tomas was involved one of the times too ..."

The only word I can manage to get out is, "What?" I sound calm.

"I'm so sorry," she says.

"I don't understand. But when we first opened ... we went to Jamaica. . . . That was our mini honeymoon. . . . We were literally in the honeymoon phase." My mind spins quickly, trying to figure out the right questions to ask. Shouldn't I be a pro at this by now? Sorting through which pertinent questions to ask about my husband's betrayals?

We were so blissfully in love when the Thirsty Owl first opened. We had been married only a few months. Marco was still plastering Facebook with our pictures.

"I'm so sorry," she says again.

We hang up. I lay down and stare at the ceiling. I wait. I wait for the meltdown, for the sobbing. Nothing comes. I know what my friend told me is true. This was the missing piece that I had been searching for. I remember reading that sociopaths cannot and will not, under any circumstances, remain faithful for longer than a few months, that even while idealizing one target, they are still constantly on the lookout for more supply. I had thought that I was the exception to this rule. I was even clinging to the thought: He was faithful for more than five years so he can't be a true sociopath. Now I know with certainty. He did not lose his mind. He conned me from the very start. He is a predator. And I am his biggest catch yet.

I put on my running sneakers and tug my sports bra over my heavy boobs. I throw on an old T-shirt and shorts and head out the front door as I call to my parents, "Going for a run. Lulu will be asleep for another hour." I jog out of Haven, taking a right on Shore Road, pumping my legs faster and faster. I wasn't sure where I was going when I first set out, but now I know. I start to pick up the pace, my lungs burn, and I gulp in cold Maine air. I focus on my breathing and my jumbled thoughts slowly untangle until the only thought in my head is *keep going.* I turn left into Fort Williams, taking a back entrance, and turn sideways to shimmy through a small opening in a fence. My eyes narrow against the sparkling water and the sun skimming the ocean. As my legs bring me closer to my destination, I want to turn back. I force myself to keep going, faster and faster. Get there, Jenny. The last part is uphill and for a second I think, *I can't do it*; my eyes water, sweat streams down my face, and my lungs burn, and then the thought fills my head, *Yes. You can. You can do anything now.* I climb the hill, lengthening my stride, pumping my arms, grunting the last few feet, and there it is. The stairs that I climbed on my wedding day lay before me. I don't stop to catch my breath; I have to keep moving or I will turn around. I climb them, remembering each step I took with my father a year ago, toward Marco. This time I am alone, and when I reach the spot where my father kissed my cheek and gave me to Marco, I finally stop. I remember how filled with love I was on that day. I remember looking at the man across from me and knowing that he would make me happy forever. And now it is time to let go of that man. Because that man never existed. There is no "old Marco" and "new Marco." Marco was always an illusion; the best magic trick I've ever seen.

SMOKE

I RUN now. Every day. Something I never thought I would say. I run, not away from the past but toward the future. Every morning I breathe in Lulu's sweet baby smell as I put her down for her morning nap, the one I can always count on for at least an hour around 9:00 A.M., and I throw on my running clothes, lace up my bright-orange sneakers, and fly out the front door. I still don't know exactly what I am running toward, but it feels good to move, to sweat, to feel my muscles straining and working. A few months ago, in the depths of the chaos and depression, my skinniest pair of pre-pregnancy jeans hung from my frame. But now I have gained back some weight, my skin glows with the summer sun, and although my stomach is soft and saggy where it used to be hard and taut, I look in the mirror and see that I look the best I have ever looked. My lips turn up in a small smile at the irony of this. I turn from the mirror and run down the stairs, wave to my mom, and head out the front door and then stop. I run back inside, grab my car keys, and yell, "Going to run some errands, be back in an hour."

Forty-five minutes later, I stare at the woman across from me. Her blonde hair hangs in a full bob just past her chin, and her eyes are clear and wise.

"What do you think?" the sleek red-headed stylist asks from behind the chair.

"I love it," I say, touching the smoothness of my hair. Suddenly, I am transported back to the bar, that first night with Marco, and I think of that girl twirling her hair nervously around her finger.

"Are you sure? You look a little sad," the stylist says with a concerned laugh.

"No, I do. I love it. Thank you." My hand goes to my hair again, and I give it a soft pat. "I was just thinking about how much there used to be."

"You needed a change, my dear."

"You have no idea."

TONIGHT I nurse my daughter to sleep. I poke the corner of her mouth gently with my finger to loosen her grip on my nipple, and she pulls away with a start. Her eyes open for a second, and one arm flails out to the side. Suddenly, for the first time, I see her. It is like I have taken off smudgy glasses that I didn't even know I was wearing. "You're so beautiful," I say in awe. "I see you." She has sandy, light-brown hair and the most beautiful blue, almond-shaped eyes I have ever seen. She smiles at me, and I say again, "Oh my God, I see you." The haze of grief that has enveloped me for six months lifts for a moment. I touch her cheek with my finger. I make a soothing, shushing sound and kiss the top of her head. Her hair smells like honey and baby, and for a moment she is the whole world and there is nothing else. I kiss her again and lay her in her crib and tiptoe out of the room, holding my breath as the door creaks in the same spot that it always creaks.

Once I'm back in my bedroom, my phone stares at me from my bedside table, beckoning me. I haven't checked either of their profiles all day. Don't do it. Don't do it. But now my fingers are moving independently from my body, typing and swiping and shaking just a tiny bit. *He can't hurt me anymore. He can't hurt me anymore. I don't even care.* This is what I tell myself. His profile shows nothing new, and my brain barely absorbs this before my fingers are already pressing and swiping toward her profile. Her profile loads, and I see she has posted a new picture. A mixture of fear, adrenaline, anxiety, and nausea mingle in my stomach as I tap once and the new picture fills the screen. And then my eyes focus, and I see . . . she is wearing my husband's pajamas. Ex-husband. *Exexexex, get it straight, Jenny.* The pajamas I bought him two Christmases ago and bought matching pairs for my dad and my sister's husband. Red and green and white stripes. Marco wore them Christmas Day and then they became his day-off pants. We would sit on the couch with Chinese takeout from across the street, him in those pj's and me in my moccasin slippers. And after we had finished our greasy meal, I would lay my head in his soft, flannel lap. A pit opens up in my heart. So now I know he can still hurt me. As I examine the picture, I feel a lump rising in my throat. I wait. The lump is still there, but I am not crying. *It's OK to cry*, I tell myself. Still, no tears. I click to my home screen and bring up my text messages.

"Croella posted a pic wearing pj's I bought Marco for Christmas. But I'm not crying."

Nat responded, "No way. Is there no limit to their asshole douchiness?? Like, NO LIMIT? But that's good. But it's OK to cry."

"I know, but now I need to stop looking. I am just digging at the wound. Need to change my behavior."

Yes. Progress. Suddenly, not crying when I see my husband's girlfriend wearing the pajamas I bought him is a step in the right direction. I laugh out loud and close my eyes.

I AM so exhausted. I am so exhausted that the word *exhausted* is almost too tiring to think, with its three goddamn syllables. Bone-numbing, eye-sockets-tingling, jaw-clenching exhaustion. It has now been six months since I have slept longer than four hours at a time. Louisa wakes only once during the night, but it segments my sleep into three- or four-hour chunks. I've tried to go to bed earlier, but my mind spins and spins until finally around midnight I slip away into a panicked, fitful sleep. My mind spins around different thoughts now that I am six months in . . . or should I say "out"? Instead of going over and over and over the details of my interactions with Marco leading up to January 20, trying to find that one that will finally make the unfathomable fathomable, or imagining him with her in our bed, imagining every detail of what must have been crazy, animalistic fucking (they broke a bed, after all), I now think of Louisa. Louisa growing up without a father. Louisa wondering if there is something fundamentally wrong with her. Louisa seeing pictures of our wedding, of us blissfully in love six months prior to her birth and thinking, no matter how many times I explain it (and how will I explain it?), *It was me. I was the reason everything fell apart.* I tell myself that Louisa will know she is so loved and she will have strong men in her life and I will tell her the (gentle, very edited) truth about what her father is and how he is flawed. And I also know deep down that there is a good chance that I will find a man who will raise her with me. A man, a good man, who will become her father through singing her to sleep, combing her hair, helping her with homework, teaching her to ride a bike, all the small moments that mean so much more than DNA. But still. My insides ache at the thought of her learning the truth about her biological father. I don't hurt as much for me anymore; I hurt for her now. And it is so much worse.

I FEEL as though I'm going backward lately. I am sick to my stomach all the time, and the anxiety is back full-force. A few days ago, I went to the mall with Louisa. She cooed in her stroller, and a group of grandparents converged on her stroller as we zipped through Macy's.

"What an absolutely beautiful baby," a white-haired woman wearing a string of pearls cried.

"My, isn't she just lovely. Enjoy!" a ruddy-cheeked, round old man called after us.

"I will," I chirped to the group, and Lulu and I, both grinning, made our way to H&M. I placed Lulu in the hallway of the dressing room area and left the door ajar to my tiny room so that I could see her the entire time. I tried on two pair of jeans and a colorful, flowy top, and the two girls in the rooms next door fawned over Lulu. "Oh my gawd, she's giving me baby fever!" said the brunette. I waltzed out of the store with the jeans and top in a bag tucked underneath the stroller, and when we pulled back into the rocky driveway of my parents' house, she was ready for a nap. I felt good, really good, and that afternoon I posted a Facebook photo of my new outfit with the caption "good f&ing riddance."

Now I am curled up in bed, my stomach twisting and turning with that familiar feeling of dread. It's as if the universe is snickering at me behind my back: *You thought you were making progress? I'll show you how weak you really are.* My appetite has disappeared again over the last couple of days, and my eyes are glazed and lifeless.

A year ago, I was in France with Marco, walking hand in hand along the cobblestone streets of a small Provençal village. Louisa, growing in my stomach, was still too small to be noticeable to passersby, and we shared the news with strangers whenever we could. "Babe, maybe you should get a size large because . . . you know." Marco placed his hand on my middle and smiled proudly at the silver-haired lady helping me pick out a handmade tunic from the racks at the Sunday market.

I thought I was done grieving this monster. I was so sure I had jumped into "recovery." But right now, lying in bed while Lulu naps, I am nowhere. I feel stuck. I am a single, thirty-one-year-old woman with a baby living in her childhood home with her retired parents. There is a constant tightness in my chest when I think about the future and how I will bridge the gap between right now and the life that is waiting for me. I say this to Lisa during one of our sessions, and she says, "That's positive movement."

"What do you mean?" I ask, surprised.

"If you're even focusing on something other than the event, the trauma, the betrayal, the heartbreak, that's positive movement forward," Lisa says, and kicks off her green loafers and curls her feet underneath her body.

"Huh. I hadn't thought of it that way. I was thinking that I'm in a really bad place right now because all of the sudden I'm coming out of my grief fog a bit, realizing, *Holy shit, what am I going to do now?*"

"Of course. You're going through the natural progression of recovery. You're moving out of complete devastation and shock, moving through the grieving process, and starting to think about the future. Do you see how huge that is? That you're even *thinking* about the future?"

My stomach unclenches for the first time in days. Being stressed, anxious, and overwhelmed is a good thing?

"But . . . ," I say, worrying aloud, "I have no applicable skills for Portland, Maine. That's something I'm starting to think about a lot. I have seven years of being an actor in New York. . . . How am I going to support myself and Louisa?" I have been living off the four credit cards I have for months now. Marco hasn't sent a single penny, and I know that I need to start working again. The thousands of dollars in debt that I have already incurred sits in the back of my mind constantly. Time is running out.

"I am sitting here, looking at a smart, beautiful, young woman. I know for a fact you will be more than OK. If you could see yourself in five years, I guarantee you that it would ease all your anxieties and stress. I know it's easy for me to sit here and say that, but I also know that it's one hundred percent true. How old are you again?"

"I'm thirty-one," I say, and wince. "Kind of old to start over."

"Are you kidding me?" Lisa says with a genuine laugh. "Thirty-one? You're so, so young. I hadn't even met my husband at your age."

I look at Lisa, surprised for a moment. I assumed she was in her early thirties or maybe even younger, and now I reevaluate. My body feels lighter as I take in her words.

"But . . . ," I say again, "I am also very anxious about the fact that my life has been completely turned upside down and I gave up my career and Marco is moving on with his life like nothing happened. As if Louisa and I don't even exist. According to Facebook, he got a fancy new job as the general manager of a chain of restaurants." I twist my fingers together and take a deep breath. "It gives me panic attacks sometimes."

"OK, hold on. You're thinking about this from your brain, your nonsociopathic brain. So yes, it's completely normal to have these thoughts and this anxiety. But here's the thing: Marco's pattern of behavior is to hurt and betray everyone, literally *everyone*, who has ever genuinely loved him. Do you think that someone like that is living a fulfilling and happy life? I know it's hard from your perspective, but when you step back and think about what you know, you can see he has a history of hurting and betraying people, you know he is a pathological liar, you know he has a pathological need to live a double life, you know he doesn't feel love or make healthy attachments . . . in the long run, who would you rather be? You or him?"

I smile. "Me. I would so much rather be me." And then, "You know, an interesting side effect of this whole experience? I'm strangely less socially anxious, like in public. Little interactions used to make me really nervous, and I would overcompensate by being super friendly. I guess I've always been a people pleaser and wanted people's approval. And now I don't give a shit. I mean, it's not like I'm mean or cold, but I'm not effusively nice or witty or charming because I want someone to like me. Like, I bought a shirt at Target the other day and talking to the cashier didn't make me nervous like it used to; we had a nice, genuine interaction and that was that. It feels strangely peaceful."

"Well, that makes a lot of sense. You're seeing other people as *real* people, separate from yourself now, with their own stories and issues, and you're probably also realizing they're not judging you or even really thinking about you because they have their own lives and problems. It sounds like you used to see strangers as self-relating, as an extension of yourself, and therefore you were worrying about what they were thinking about you. Now, you're realizing most people have their own lives to think about and aren't spending their time thinking about yours."

"You're right, I guess that's true," I say, crossing one leg over the other. "I feel like I keep going back and forth between emotions. Sometimes I feel OK. Sometimes I feel right back to square one. When am I really going to be 'recovered'?" I ask anxiously.

"You are the kind of person who likes to identify the problem and solve it in the most efficient way possible, yes?" Lisa asks with a smile.

"Yes," I agree.

"Well, unfortunately, this process is not going to be linear. I know you want a list that you can go through and check off and be done with: 'denial,' 'sadness,' 'anger.' But that's not the way it works. It's not so clean. However, I can tell you this: You are doing the hard work right now. What you're *not* doing is running into another relationship, hoping that you can skip over a bunch of steps by burying yourself in someone else. That's when women start getting into really bad patterns and really bad situations." She looks at me intently. "It might not feel like it, but you *are* doing the deep work and living the process. You have to trust that. What we might want to start thinking about, what you might be *ready* to start thinking about is: What drew you to Marco in the first place?"

"You mean like, what part of it was my fault?" I ask apprehensively.

"No," Lisa says forcefully. "That's not what I'm getting at. What I'm getting at is you understanding what parts of you were drawn to someone like Marco. If you can do that inner work, if you can start to become aware of those parts of yourself, that is when you will start to take back your power."

I stop for a moment, considering my answer. What was it that Marco saw in me that I didn't see in myself?

"I liked feeling like I was part of a fairy tale," I say slowly. "I liked feeling adored."

Lisa nods as if she knew what I would say. "What's interesting, though, is that you were able to ignore or filter out a lot of data at the beginning of your relationship with Marco. Such as him having a girlfriend and him lying to and hurting someone else. You were able to twist that around in your mind to fit your agenda. I think that's what we want to start concentrating on. How you mold or filter data in order to serve your version of reality."

"Oh God." I cross my arms tightly. "This is hard."

We spend the rest of the session talking about how I pick and choose what I want to see and how I reject data that does not fit my paradigm. Lisa says that everyone does this to a certain extent but that, for some reason, I have a tendency to filter data to an extreme that has proven to be detrimental. I've always thought of myself as an optimist, but now I'm starting to wonder about the difference between being "optimistic" and being delusional. I was so eager to believe in the fairy tale that I blinded myself to some serious character flaws. I was so bound to my belief that Marco was "the one" that I took in all the "good" (love bombing, intense feelings, sexual chemistry) and rejected the "bad" (lying, cheating, a dark, murky past).

"It's like within a few weeks you had already decided that you and Marco were going to be together forever and so any data that clashed with that reality, you just threw away." Lisa pauses for a moment as I take this in. "Those first months of dating are supposed to be kind of a trial period, to determine whether you like the other person and want to be with him."

"Oh, Jesus, that's so true. At the time, it felt like . . . it truly felt like life and death." I think about how building a sense of self and having boundaries are so important and how I had never consciously developed either before. For the first time in my life, my thoughts and feelings and actions are all beginning to align with one another. It seems like such a simple concept, but now, if someone or something doesn't make me feel good, doesn't bring me joy or fulfill me in some way, I simply don't engage. Before, so eager to please everyone around me, I had never stopped to take stock of how *I* really felt or what *I* really wanted. It is incredibly freeing to invest in what nourishes your emotional well-being and stop engaging with the people and things that make you feel less than. Somehow, I never realized that I always had a choice in creating my own reality.

I leave Lisa's office and walk in the hot sun to the coffee shop on the corner. I still feel the anxiety in my chest, and it travels around my body, making pit stops in my head and stomach, but now I feel something else mingling, knocking around tentatively. I get in line behind three other people waiting to order coffee and hold on to this new feeling making its way through my body. What is it? I move up to the counter and am about to give my order to the hipster at the cash register when suddenly I realize, it's hope.

"A small latte, please," I say with a smile, and the boy gives me a big smile back and I take in the smallness of this encounter, focusing on the warmth passing between us. A year ago, I would have smiled brightly and felt vaguely anxious: *What does he think about me? Does he think I'm nice? I better be extra polite to make up for that rude lady in front of me.* Now, I have no room for those feelings. I look at the boy as he takes my five-dollar bill and makes change and wonder what his story is, is he a student at the Maine College of Art working a summer job to pay for tuition, far from home and adjusting to living on his own and all the small freedoms and responsibilities that go along with it?

"Thank you," I say gently, looking him in the eyes, as he hands me back two quarters and a dime.

"Have a nice day," he says.

"You, too."

———

THAT afternoon, my phone lights up on my bedside table, and I see the name "Marco." My stomach plummets. I've been in "no contact" for weeks now, but his unpredictable texts still come in and jolt me into a panic. I reach over and swipe the text open.

"I was going to end that waitress. She took advantage of me while I was drunk, and I was so scared about her telling you."

What is he talking about? What waitress? He must somehow

know that my friend called and told me about the women from the Thirsty Owl. My heart speeds up. Before I know what I'm doing, I break no contact and type back, "What do you mean 'end'?"

"I was going to execute her. I was going to push her down the stairs at the restaurant. No one would have known."

I stare at the text. *Execute.* I pause and take stock of how this makes me feel. I am not afraid. I am not sad. I feel something, but I can't put my finger on it. I get chills. I am about to reply again when I hear Lulu waking up from her nap. I power my phone off instead.

———

AN hour later, I walk through the aisles of Target pushing Lulu in her stroller. My mom and her sister, my aunt Julia, are meeting me to do a bit of shopping, and I have arrived a few minutes early. I walk slowly past racks of clothes, taking in the huge, empty store. After living in New York for nine years, I am still not used to having personal space in public, and I luxuriate in the unapologetic suburban consumerism.

"Oh look, Mags, I see them!" I hear the familiar ring of my aunt's voice travel from the entrance of the store to the rack of clothing where I am holding up a striped tank top against my body. She was one of the first people I told about the real reason I was home. After a month of my parents dodging questions about why Louisa and I were in Maine for such a long visit, she came over for coffee and donuts at the end of March. I sat with Louisa in a chair at the head of the dining table and nervously picked at the donut in front of me.

"Aunt Julia, I have to tell you something," I said, swallowing down the lump in my throat. "The real reason I'm home with Louisa is because I found out Marco was having an affair when Louisa was a few weeks old, and I've moved home until I figure out what to do." I stared into my coffee, and when I looked up my aunt's face was bright red, tears streaming down her nose and cheeks. She sank into a chair, and for several minutes all she could get out was "What?" over and over. When I saw that she was crying, I let myself cry, too—big, ugly sobs. And then my mom started to cry and hugged my aunt.

"But your wedding was just a few months ago," my aunt finally said. "I don't understand."

"Join the club," I said with a small smile, drying my eyes with a napkin. I explained the e-mail, the change in personality, his numbness, and the suicide attempt.

I had completely forgotten that when my cousin Luke was a baby, my aunt's abusive husband had disappeared one day with all their money and had never come back. She had remarried my uncle Sam a few years later, and everyone in our family had buried the first part of her story in a deep hole and thrown twenty years of new memories on top of it. She told me how hard the next few years would be but that I would be OK. "You have to grieve the family and the future you thought you would have. And you have to go through an entire cycle of holidays, birthdays, and seasons before you really stop feeling that raw pain. Even then, all the 'firsts' will be hard, the first time she sleeps in her crib, her first word, the first time she walks. But then one day you will wake up and you will be so glad it happened. And that it happened when she was a newborn. You will realize your lives are so, so much better without Marco, if this is really who he is."

I absorbed her words and stored them away, aware that I would need to draw on them one day. After that morning, when I was able to leave the house for a few hours at a time before the wave would crash down on me, the three of us (four of us counting a gurgling baby) met for coffee at Panera every couple of weeks. Eventually, I told Julia some of the horrific details and showed her pictures of Marco's new girlfriend.

Now I watch her fiery red hair over the clothing racks and marvel, as I do every time I see my mom and my aunt together, at the physical differences between the two sisters. It has been a family joke for as long as I can remember that my aunt, petite and curvy with bright red hair, was a product of the milkman. Secretly I have always wondered if there is some truth to this joke. It is not only the physical differences that give me pause. My aunt is a vivacious firecracker, legendary for her dirty jokes and emotional outbursts, while my mom is calm and spiritual, the steady ocean that our family glides on.

"There's my beautiful girl," my aunt Julia says, wrapping me in a hug. "Or should I say beautiful *girls*," Julia says with a cackle, and makes a kissy face at Louisa.

"More like beautiful *babes*," my mom says, and they look at each other and suddenly they are two sisters laughing together and the milkman thought dissolves.

"I have something really disturbing to tell you," I say as we head toward the baby aisles.

"Excuse me? *More* disturbing information? Is that even *possible* at this point?"

"Apparently Marco is the gift that keeps on giving," I say with a wry smile, and then tell her about the phone call I received a week ago.

Aunt Julia had stopped mid-step at some point during my revelation and now she stands stock-still. "Look at my arm," she says, raising her arm in front of my face. "I have *goosebumps.*"

"Crazy, right?" I say.

"So this was going on the entire time? The cheating? Wait, wait, wait, so he had cheated *before* your wedding?" Julia says, furrowing her brow.

"Dozens of times, probably," I say. "If he was *caught* those three times."

Julia shivers and then starts walking again. "Oh my God," she says, suddenly stopping. She leans into my ear on her tiptoes and says in a hushed whisper, "I bet he had sex with his friend Tomas, too!"

She is so serious that I choke back laughter, raise my eyebrows, and whisper back conspiratorially, "probably."

But her suggestion sticks in my mind as we fill the cart with formula and diapers. I take out my phone and bring up Marco's Instagram profile. I click the photo that has been in the back of my mind since he posted it two days ago. A selfie shot from above, lying on a beach towel, his chest and face slick with greasy tanning oil, making the straight male equivalent of a duckface. "Catching some rays," the caption reads.

The person in this photo was so foreign to me, so unlike the person I knew and married, that I could barely look at it before I had to turn away.

Suddenly, I remember reading about vore. *Of course,* I think. *Psychopaths desire to be consumed whole by someone else because they lack an identity themselves.* Psychopaths mirror other individuals so completely that in a sense it *is* like they are being swallowed whole by their target, until they turn the tables and rip their target apart from the inside out. Maybe the desire to fill the void, to obtain an identity, manifests itself in this sexual vore fantasy of being fully consumed by someone else.

I look at the photo again. Of course. He's turning into a male version of Croella.

It is like I am actually watching him cross over; I am watching his physical and emotional transformation into someone else entirely. For a few months, he ping-ponged between two people— the person I knew, the guy he called "old Marco," and the money-obsessed, club-going, selfie-taking person, the "new" Marco. Now I see very clearly that two personas were battling inside him over the last few months; he hadn't fully transitioned from the person he became because of me to the person he was becoming in order to control Croella. I look at the photo for as long as I can stomach and then slip my phone into my jeans' back pocket.

Aunt Julia wanders into the shoe aisles, and I sidle up to my mom. "Another thing, Mom. Marco texted me today that he was planning to 'execute' the waitress from the Thirsty Owl that he slept with." I push the stroller steadily forward. "Because he was worried about her telling me. He said he could have done it and 'no one would have known.'" I make air quotes with my fingers. "He just sent me this text totally out of nowhere. Isn't that creepy as you-know-what?"

"Are you serious?" My mom comes to a standstill in the middle of the diaper aisle.

I laugh. "I mean, we know he's full of shit at this point. The crazy thing is I barely flinched when I got that text. I just roll my eyes when I get those kinds of texts from him now."

"But, Jenny, why do you think he sent that to you?" my mom says it in a way that makes it clear I'm missing something.

"To . . . scare me?" I try to come up with the correct answer.

"And why would that scare you?" my mom prods.

"It scares me because . . ." We start to walk again slowly down the aisle. "It scares me because he's telling me he was planning to kill someone who was in his way." I pause a moment as the full realization comes flooding in. "And that's me now."

"Yes, that's you now. In his mind, you're the reason for his fall from grace. Not his actions, not what he did, but that you caught him," my mom says, finishing my thought.

"Jesus Christ. But the thing is, when he was truly backed into a corner, he didn't hurt me or Louisa. He tried to hurt himself . . . or wanted to make it look that way. So I'm not super worried." I pop a few Puffs into Lulu's outstretched hand. "I've read that the majority of psychopaths aren't violent."

"Well, I thank God every day that the three of you didn't go to Peaks." My mom shakes her head.

"What do you mean?"

"Jenny," my mom says pointedly. "A cottage on a remote island in the middle of the winter." She looks at me like what she's saying is completely obvious.

I laugh. "You think he would have done something? To me and Louisa?"

"Accidents happen," my mom says completely seriously, and a chill runs through my body. I remember the way Marco came toward me in the kitchen when I tried to flee to Maine, his eyes dark and empty. But still, in all the years we were together he never once showed any violent tendencies.

"No way," I say, but I've stopped laughing. "I mean, I really don't think so."

"Well, I'm glad you didn't go. I'm so glad you didn't go."

———

I HAVE started applying to jobs while Louisa naps. There is part of me that is scared shitless to start working again and part of me that is thrilled. My résumé consists of seven years of acting in New York and a couple of years as a paralegal and an analyst at a hedge fund. I spent an hour buffing and glossing my résumé with temp work that I did during my pregnancy. It is not much but it is something, and apparently my résumé looks credible enough because today I have my first interview for a paralegal position at a small law firm. *You're not ready yet*, a small voice whispers in my ear. *You're still having panic attacks on a daily basis.* I shake my head and say "*shh*" out loud while I dab on blush and mascara in the mirror. I pull on the black, knee-length pencil skirt my sister has let me borrow. I glance back in the mirror. In my high-waisted black skirt and tucked in silk blouse I look svelte, but when I poke at my middle my fingers sink into a soft pouch leftover from pregnancy and rapid weight loss. "Ugh," I say, grabbing the skin and pulling. Throughout my pregnancy, especially at the end, I fretted over how difficult it would be to lose all the weight I had gained. I never thought that I would have the opposite problem. I lost too much weight too fast, and now I have a loose pouch only around my middle. "Not a diet I would recommend," I say out loud to my reflection. I twist my hair into a knot on the top of my head and step into black heels I bought at DSW last week.

"Wow, you look great. Good luck!" my parents call as I walk through the kitchen to the garage.

"Thank you," I say nervously, and kiss Louisa on the head before I leave.

My stomach flips and flops on the drive into the Old Port. The interview is at a small law firm housed in a quaint brick building on a cobblestone street.

"Hi, my name is Jen. I have an interview. I'm a bit early," I say with what I hope is calm self-possession, as I try to keep my voice steady.

"Hi! Sure, I'll let them know. You can take a seat while you wait. Great outfit, by the way," the young receptionist chirps before picking up her ringing phone.

I smile big in acknowledgment and take a deep breath. I can do this.

Sitting at a large conference table, across from the four founding partners, I quickly gain confidence. They are young, early to late thirties, and they talk to me as a peer. I explain that I have moved back to Maine because I had a baby. I am looking forward to going back to work after spending six months at home as a full-time mom. I say it with a knowing smile, as if it has been hard but rewarding—as if I didn't discover that my husband was a psychopath when our baby was a month old. They all nod and smile knowingly back.

By the end of the interview I know that I will receive a second interview, and I get a callback e-mail before I have even turned off Shore Road onto Haven. Yes. Yes. Yes.

BURN

A FEW people who have experienced deep loss themselves have asked me, "Are you in the anger stage yet?" And when I respond, "I don't know. . . ." they say, "You'll know." Deep down I have always been quite certain that I am just not an angry person, and the anger that I feel will always be covered with love and heartbreak like a rock covered in moss. And then suddenly, out of nowhere, today, the day after my interview, I *know*.

I am livid.

I am *outraged*.

How. Fucking. Dare. He.

I walk around and around and around the loop, practicing conversations with him in my mind where I say all the things I should have said on January 20. I let this anger swirl around inside me for days. It has nowhere to go. I tell myself to rise above and that this is good; I am making progress. And then it pours out in a series of texts to Marco. I break no contact to send him picture after picture of the most unflattering pictures of Croella I can find online with hashtag #stupidman, #youfuckedup!!!, and #goodchoice. It is low and it is callous and I am so much better than this and it feels fan-fucking-tastic. This goes on for days. Marco responds with an "OK, Jen," half the time and love-bombing the other half. ("All I ever wanted was a family. All I wanted was to wake up next to you every morning.")

I'm afraid I am stuck in this anger. It feels better than what I was feeling before, and I don't want to let it go, but it is so heavy and I drag it around with me wherever I go. It is consuming me. When I wring my hands together and tell Lisa, she looks at me like, "Yeah, what did you expect?" and says, "You're going to be angry for a long time. I mean, look at your life right now. Look at the narrative that he created for your daughter's birth. You have a lot of anger to process." We talk about tools that can help me get to the other side, such as cutting down on checking their profiles on social media and reading books on trusting my intuition.

"I want you to rebuild trust in your own inner compass," Lisa says. "You have good instincts, but for some reason you pushed those instincts way down and ignored them. You said you felt sick to your stomach for weeks at the beginning of your relationship with Marco and same thing with the Thirsty Owl. Something inside you was saying, 'Whoa, hold on, this doesn't add up,' but you ignored that voice and plowed on. What we need to figure out is why and start to arm you with some concrete tools that you can draw on until you truly learn to listen to your intuition."

This sounds good in theory, but I am skeptical. I can't stop. I want to hurt them, both of them, so badly. I want them to pay. This afternoon is my follow-up interview with the law firm. I get ready and sit on my bed staring at my phone. The anger that is coursing through my body feels so good. I am going to get a fancy job, and we will be fine. Ha. *Fuck you, Marco.* I send off a new series of pictures. My head is dizzy with adrenaline and anger. I am waiting for something. Some kind of vindication. His response lights up my screen. "At least she knows how to make a man happy." Suddenly, my anger is wiped away by a flood of tears. I try to hold onto my anger, to pull it back in, but it has already drifted so far downstream that I am left stranded at the mouth of the river. I pick up Louisa and trudge downstairs. I hide my face behind her soft hair and murmur into her ear that I love her and that I'm going to try to do better for her.

"What happened?" my dad asks sharply as soon as he sees my face.

"Oh, nothing. I texted Marco some stupid, mean things. I wanted him to feel like an idiot for choosing her over us. But it didn't work. He just texted back 'At least she knows how to make a man happy.'" I get to the last word and start to cry again. "I know that after everything he's done, I should be used to it, but stuff like that still hurts. I just want him to pay. I want to hurt him like he's hurt me." My voice comes out in broken sobs, and my mom hugs me and then gently takes Louisa.

"You can't hurt him, Jenny," my dad says. "You can't hurt someone who has no feelings. No matter what you try to do to hurt him, he will come back and hurt you worse. That is what he does. He hurts women. He doesn't hurt them physically, but he has a very finely sharpened set of tools that he uses to hurt women. He is a master at this. It comes as naturally to him as breathing, and he derives great pleasure from it. Every time you text him an insult, you feed his ego, you energize him. This is fun for him." My dad says this quickly and matter-of-factly. "Maybe your therapist is right that he doesn't even know what he's doing, that it's subconscious, but now that we know that he was cheating throughout your entire relationship, we know that he was never even trying to be a good guy. He never had good intentions." My dad clenches and unclenches his jaw. "You need to understand one very simple fact: He is feeding off your pain."

I know that my dad is right. I will only break free when I no longer care. I run to my bathroom and splash cold water on my face. I redo my makeup quickly for my interview. I glance at myself. Passable. I hurry back downstairs and out the door. "Bye," I yell.

"Good luck," two voices yell back simultaneously. I run back inside and kiss Lulu.

Somehow I make it through the second interview. I meet one of the partners who was in court during my first interview. He is cute and nice and shy. His eyes don't move down my body, and he doesn't flirt. He tells me that his wife is on maternity leave with their three-month-old right now and that his paternity leave will start as soon as she goes back to work. He is the kind of man I would have found utterly boring before. As I shake his hand on my way out, I think, *Why, why couldn't I have picked someone like you?*

———

AS I begin opening up to other women, I notice something: Every woman I share tidbits of my story with has her own account to tell—either tentatively, cautiously disclosing a painful event, or furiously, voraciously spitting out the story that has been on the tip of her tongue for years—something that either happened to her or someone close to her.

First, there was Ava, a friend from New York. Ava is uniquely, breathtakingly beautiful, with smooth dark skin; an abundance of black, curly hair; and deep brown eyes. I remember being surprised by how friendly, eager to please, and helpful she came across the first time I met her. She had moved from the UK to New York a few months prior to the first time we met. She relocated for her acting career, and we bumped into each other at the agency we were both signed with. We became fast friends that day in our agent's small office, after realizing quickly that we shared the same doubts, fears, and aspirations about our careers (or lack thereof). It probably didn't hurt that we were the opposite physical types and knew instinctively we would never be competing for a role. We began hanging out, drinking wine at my apartment, coaching each other before auditions, and venting after particularly horrific ones. She had been calling me and leaving messages every few days ever since I fled to Maine. I put off calling her back, instead shooting off texts here and there: "I'm OK. I can't talk yet. I'll call when I can." The very thought of calling exhausted me and sent a shiver of panic through my body. But she kept calling. And texting. And finally I realized this girl I had known for only a year was silently rooting for me and was not going anywhere. A few weeks ago, around the time I began interviewing, I was suddenly compelled to reach out to my friend who had proven so supportive.

"Ava," I said, "I'm sorry I haven't called until just now."

"Love," she said, "tell me everything." So I did, starting from the beginning. When I told her about my sociopath research, there was silence for a moment.

"Jen. I've just had a bloody epiphany," she said, her soft British clip came through the phone. "I think my father is a sociopath."

I quickly remembered back to her telling me off the cuff, after several glasses of white wine, that her father was currently on his fifth wife. The revelation had shocked me, but she laughed it off and we never dipped any deeper into her past.

"My dad had an affair when I was two and my brother was a baby," she told me over the phone. "My mum called the hotel he was staying at on a business trip, and his pretty young colleague picked up. It was late at night, and my mom knew right away." Ava went on, half to me, half to herself, piecing it together for the first time. "She told me when I was a teenager that she hung up the phone and then leaned over and threw up into the sink. She was devastated. My dad promised it was a terrible mistake and that he would end it. He begged for another chance. She had two babies and had just spent all her money putting him through law school, so she forgave him. And then two years later, when she finally felt they were on solid ground again, he packed a suitcase and walked next door . . . to his mistress's house." Ava let out a cold laugh. "My mum finally understood why my dad had insisted on moving the family right after he had supposedly ended his affair."

I was silent for a moment, digesting this information.

"But," I started, "you said he was on his fifth wife?"

"Oh, yes, he married the mistress and then left her for another woman a few years later. And then again. And again and again. All these years I just thought he was a womanizer, and my mum spent many, many years blaming herself for the end of their marriage. But the relationship cycle you were talking about? He's done it to all of his wives. And, Jen," she said slowly, "I think he's done it to me."

We talked for another hour about what it was like growing up in and out of her dad's good graces: Always trying to be on her father's "good side" but always feeling vaguely like she and her brother were just trophies that he would parade around when it suited him.

And there was Monica, the woman who ran the coffee and pastry counter at the small community center on Peaks Island, who told me that she had been happily engaged to the man of her dreams five years earlier. They had dated for a year and bought a house together before he proposed. She went to visit her sister across the country who had just had a baby. When she came home, she walked up to her front door and found it locked, which was odd because her and her fiancé never locked the door. She fished inside her purse for the key that she had almost never used, but the key wouldn't even fit in the hole, let alone open the door. So she pulled her phone out to call her fiancé and that's when she saw she had a voice mail.

"I listened to the message five times before it made any sense at all—before it sank in. He only said it was over and that he had changed the lock to the house. That was all. He never picked up my calls, and I never talked to him again—except through law-yers. Oh, and another woman moved in the next week. With her two kids." Monica paused and smiled at Louisa. "I know you won't believe me now, but this is the best thing that could have ever hap-pened to you."

And then there was Delaney. Delaney. A woman who had

popped into the back of my mind on January 20 and stayed there, just under the surface, floating beneath the waves of depression and anger and fear. A woman I had been trying to forget ever since I met her two years earlier. It was the first hair-modeling gig I had ever booked. L'Oréal had hired me to showcase their new line of hair-color products. They were going to dye my dirty blonde hair a shocking red to turn my drab "before" into a stunning and fierce "after." Delaney was my makeup artist that day, and I liked her immediately. Her classically beautiful face, complete with elegant, long blonde hair and a perfect button nose, contrasted with her brash and colorful personality. While she did my makeup, we talked. I gushed about being engaged to Marco, the Argentinian father who had appeared out of nowhere and swept me off my feet. At the time, the Thirsty Owl was just on the horizon, and I talked excitedly about the possibility that we would be restaurant owners soon.

"I was married to a Cuban guy," she said, concentrating on the eye shadow she swept across my lids. "I fell for him hard. I mean, *hard*. He was gorgeous and so charming. I got him his green card."

I listened carefully, not moving a muscle.

"While we were married, I started a makeup line, and it became really successful. My husband didn't work, but for some reason that never bothered me. He was so supportive, and I was making plenty of money from my company. Anyway, right after he got his ten-year green card, I found out he was cheating on me. With, like, a dozen women."

"Oh my God. What? That's so fucked up," I gasped as Delaney dabbed blush onto my cheeks.

"I'm not trying to scare you," she said, tapping her makeup brush against her palette.

"Oh no." I laughed loudly. "Marco would never ever cheat. I mean, thank you for sharing your story, but no." I laughed again, too loudly. "Just trust me, it's completely different. He's my best friend; he's really my other half. He would never do anything like that." I changed the subject quickly.

Her story had been running through my mind since January 20, rising closer and closer to the surface, until finally, after talking to Ava, I e-mailed Delaney.

I don't know if you remember me—you did my makeup for a L'Oréal photo shoot. I had a baby a few months ago. When my daughter was a month old, I found out my husband had a girlfriend. You told me about something similar that happened to you. I'm not sure exactly why I'm e-mailing you. I just felt like maybe you told me your story for a reason and I wanted to reach out. Jen

Within hours her response appeared: *"HOLY SHIT girl. Call me."*

"First, tell me everything," she said as soon as she picked up. After I brought her up to speed, she said, "You know, I wasn't sure why I told you my story when I met you. I had barely told anyone what happened at that point. I just felt compelled to tell you. There was something about the way you talked about Marco. I can't explain it. I felt I needed to warn you." Delaney then told me the part of the story she left out two years ago. As part of the divorce settlement, she had to pay her husband $500,000, half of what her company was worth. She had just finished paying him alimony a few months earlier.

"Wait, what do you mean? Why did you have to pay him when he was the one who cheated?" I asked in shock.

"New York is a no-fault state. That means it doesn't matter why you're getting divorced; you split the marital property fifty-fifty. And my company was considered marital property since I started it during the marriage. I ended up selling the company and paying him half. I had to completely start over with a brand-new company, which is now building momentum and becoming even more successful than the first line. It was that or he would continue to own half of my makeup brand forever. And since I was the bread-winner, I've been paying him monthly alimony for five years."

"Wow . . . fuck," was all I could get out.

"So in a way you're lucky that you don't have much in the way of marital assets. It seems like all Marco left you with is debt. I know that doesn't seem lucky, but trust me, it's a good thing. It will make the divorce much, much easier." Delaney went on to tell me that once she got through the divorce and over her heartbreak, she realized how ridiculous the whole relationship had been. "I mean, I'm smart. I'm from a good family. I have a lot to offer, and I picked this dude because I felt sorry for him? And because I wanted to, like, lift him up or some shit? Honey"—her voice boomed through the phone strong and loud—"when you come out on the other side of this, the amount of power you walk away with is going to blow your fucking mind."

TRUTH LIKE FIRE

IT has been about a month since I have had any contact with Marco. I feel good. I have taken a part-time job at a small financial planning company. Louisa will go into day care three days a week. After the cost of day care, I will take home exactly fifty-eight dollars a week, but it's a way to transition back into the workforce and, more than that, back into life.

My phone lights up on my bedside table, and I glance at it out of the corner of my eye. It's a text from Nat: "Wow, he's really going for it, eh?"

"Going for what?" I suddenly feel nauseated.

"Oh no, I thought you'd have seen by now. His Facebook profile picture."

At the same time, I receive a text from Holly that reads, "Hey my friend, stay strong. Remember, you are the better person and the best revenge is to not let him affect you." Holly and Stella from the beginning have taken the same stance: Yes, Marco is a Grade A dickwad, but turning the other cheek is, in the long run, the best for Louisa and me.

I tap the Facebook icon on my phone and type "Marco Medina" into the search bar. Even though we are no longer Facebook friends, I can still see his public profile picture. For a moment my brain doesn't register what I am seeing. A shirtless man drapes his arm around a woman in a bikini on the bow of a yacht. She kisses his cheek. He holds a cocktail in one hand. Her long blonde hair covers her face almost completely. His hair is greased back. Her legs are crossed into an unnatural position that reminds me of Betty Boop. His face is pursed into a smug smile. For several minutes, I stare at the image on my phone. After six months of Marco denying the existence of this relationship, this feels like seeing the Easter Bunny riding a unicorn. There are two comments. I click them with a trembling thumb.

"Noooooo???" from his dad. Oh, Oscar. I ache for him for half a second before my eyes travel to the next comment. "You DO know adultery is a misdemeanor, right?" from one of his best friends.

"Oh my God." I breathe. I sit staring at the picture. Comment after comment comes in, half of them condemning Marco and half of them totally clueless that the blonde in the picture is not me. I can't look away. I click refresh over and over. "Look at mommy!! Woohoo!!" writes an old coworker of ours. Jesus Christ. A few minutes later, a picture of Andrew's gleaming bald head appears and his reply reads, "That's not mommy, my friend." The next time I click refresh, all the comments have disappeared.

I can't look away.

I click refresh again and my stomach drops. Five new comments. How is that even possible? I click the comments and they open. For a second, I'm not sure what I am looking at. I see Oscar's first comment "Noooooo???" followed by Marco's friend's adultery comment over and over. For a split second, I wonder if Facebook has been infected with a magical virus, and it is spitting out the deleted comments over and over. And then I scroll up and see Holly's tiny face above each screenshot. Holly is posting screenshots of the deleted comments faster than Marco can delete. For every screenshot that Marco deletes, Holly posts two more until there are eleven new comments and "Noooooo???" and "You DO know adultery is a misdemeanor, right?" unravels down his Facebook page like a spool of yarn. Finally, the comments once again disappear one by one until the picture stands alone like a shining beacon of sleaziness.

"I'm sorry dude. I just fucking snapped," Holly texts me.

I love her.

That night dozens of texts and Facebook messages come in. Everyone who either didn't know what had happened or were waiting for an obvious moment to contact me do so tonight. "Wtf!" "He makes me want to vomit." "Scum of the Earth." "Don't waste your time on them. The sooner you don't think about them at all, the better. Let them dig their own graves," they say.

These past few days I have felt something growing inside me. At first I thought it was my good friend anger. But it is not anger; it feels similar, but there is something different about it. I concentrate on the feeling and let it grow. I know what it is. It is bloodlust. I want revenge. I can taste it; the metallic tang on the tip of my tongue. There is a storm brewing; the gathering winds whip my insides. I understand now that the truth, like fire, starts as a tiny ember. At first, I could see only billows of smoke. Temporarily blinded, I stumbled, tightly closing my stinging eyes. But then the ember began to catch and the fire grew. Flame by flame, it rose. The smoke surrounding me began to lift. The fire raged. My body grew hot, and, suddenly, the air was pure. My eyes opened, bright and clear. Now that the fire is inside me, I can't go back. I know deep in my bones that, eventually, the Universe will do its thing. Marco and the Croatian will destroy themselves; they will implode into a million shards of bad decisions.

For every woman who has been cast aside like yesterday's trash after placing her life in the hands of the man she trusts. For every woman who has a child with a man who thinks parenting is taking "the kid" to the movies once a month. For every woman who sighs to herself and thinks, *Karma will get him in the end*. For every woman who has been cheated on, taken advantage of, deceived, taken for granted, betrayed. This next part is for you.

RISE

Nervous, but feeling alive, energized even, I sit outside Lisa's office, waiting for her to peek her head out her door and call me in. It has been six months since the first time I sat in Lisa's office, staring at the whip-smart, put-together woman across from me and thinking wistfully, *I used to be like you*. I bounce my knee rhythmically while I wait and fidget with a necklace Stella gave me. A small blue stone, Louisa's birthstone, set on a simple gold chain.

"Jen?" She smiles, and I stand up quickly, grabbing my purse off the seat beside me and slipping into the office.

"How are you?" Lisa asks, settling into her armchair.

"I'm OK," I say. My foot taps the floor. I take a deep breath. "Actually, I'd like to talk to you about something." Here goes. "I've been thinking the past few weeks about something more and more. And I have this idea that's taking shape. It's feeling good, like it's coming from a really grounded place." Lisa looks at me encouragingly. An idea has been circulating in my head for weeks, but I pushed it down. *It's unrealistic,* I thought. *It'll take too much time.* Finally, I decided to listen to what my intuition was trying to tell me. I let it live in my head for a while, burrowing deeper and deeper, taking root in every cell of my body.

"The more I think about it, the more I am gravitating toward something." I take another deep breath. "I think I want to become some sort of therapist or counselor and specialize in personality disorders—or, rather, helping women recover from sociopathic relationships." The last words come out in a rush of excitement. I brace myself for Lisa to laugh. Or gently tell me that I'm way too fucked up to ever be able to help someone else. Instead, she sits straight up in her chair. "*Yes,*" she says. "Yes. Yes. Yes. I've been waiting for this. OK, let's talk."

Encouraged, I ask her carefully about her own background, not sure what kind of privacy issues she might have as a therapist. She dives right in.

"So there are two paths to becoming a licensed therapist. You can either get your LCSW or your LCPC." She explains to me what these initials stand for: Licensed Clinical Social Worker and Licensed Clinical Professional Counselor. I scribble notes furiously in my notebook as she talks. She explains that the master's program she did met on-campus only during the summer, from June to August, and then during the fall, winter, and spring you do your fieldwork wherever you want.

"Can you get paid fieldwork?" I ask hopefully. I have to start making money. I've been living off credit cards for months now. Luckily, I don't pay rent, and until recently Louisa's needs were mostly met by my body. Soon, though, we will need a place of our own, and I will need to prove that I can support myself and my daughter.

I understand better now why women stay with men in horrific, abusive situations, especially with small children involved. It would seem as though a woman would leave an abusive situation to protect her children. But those first few months, I was barely functioning, so deeply immersed in the pain of losing Marco and the future I thought I would have. I couldn't eat, I couldn't sleep, I shook with anxiety. I placed Louisa's well-being in the hands of my parents. I knew she was safe and that I could safely go through the necessary emotions, the grief, the withdrawal, the anger. But what about women without support systems? Without the means to leave?

"Unfortunately, no, it's all unpaid internships for three years. But, you could have your own practice in three years."

We talk about other master's in social work programs and master's in counseling programs, too. There are a couple of decent ones in Maine, and I'm surprised to learn that a lot of good master's programs are offered online. I leave Lisa's office excited. Yes. I am actually excited about something. I remember six months ago, thinking, *I will never laugh my high-pitched hyena laugh again.* The laugh that came out naturally before I could stop it. A free, full-body, two-toned shriek. And then it happened a few weeks ago. I don't even remember what spurred it, but I remember so clearly thinking, *Oh my God, my real laugh!* As I skip out of Lisa's office, I have that same feeling but even deeper. Somewhere along the way, I had stopped feeling excited for myself and only felt excited for Marco. I lived vicariously through his achievements, his pleasures, his dreams. I have a lovely, grounded, deep-in-my-bones feeling of excitement for myself and for Louisa. I want to show her what strength is, that it's OK to stumble, hell, it's OK to fall on your fucking ass. Eventually, you will get back up. I want to inspire her. I want to teach her that sometimes it takes going through hell to find yourself. I want her to know that she doesn't have to fix anyone, or give a part of herself away in order to love someone else. And I want her to know that she, *she*, is the reason that I got this amazing chance to create the life I was meant to live. Our life.

I WAKE up to silence and immediately roll over to check the time. It is 6:30 A.M. No squawks yet from Louisa's room. I luxuriously stretch my arms and legs, pointing my feet and wiggling my toes beneath the down comforter. I flick on the table lamp and let my pupils adjust to the bright rays of light. I wonder if I can sneak into the bathroom and brush my teeth before Lulu wakes up. I slowly lower one leg to the floor and then the other and take one tiptoe step toward the bathroom when I hear a high-pitched burst of sound. Seb is visiting for the first time since we left New York, and he's sleeping in my old room, right next door. I don't want Louisa to wake him, so I change my course and patter into Lulu's room.

"Do I hear a happy baby?" I whisper as I open the door slowly and peek my head around the edge. "Why yes, I do hear a baby!" A bouncing Lulu clutches the end of the crib and gurgles. Her face lights up in a big gummy smile as I move toward her, and she lets out a celebratory shriek of being found. I unzip her sleep sack and scoop her from the crib. "Hello, animals," I say to the mobile hanging from the ceiling. "*Un, deux, trois, quatre, cinq,*" I recite softly to the five stars draped across the window. I nuzzle my mouth and nose in Louisa's hair and breathe in her soapy honey smell. "Come watch me brush my teeth," I tell her, and carry her into the bathroom and plunk her down on the floor. She stares at me as I prepare my toothbrush, and then her face breaks into a smile as I brush. "I know," I say through toothpaste, and spit, "it's pretty funny."

I hoist her back onto my hip, and we trudge down the stairs and into the kitchen, where my parents are already bustling around. My mom pours steaming coffee into a mug, and my dad unloads the dishwasher.

"Lulu!!!" they both cry, and in response Louisa smiles with her whole face and bounces against my hip. It is Sunday morning. It is the last few weeks of summer, and the temperature hovers near eighty degrees mid-day but has started to drop in the mornings and at night—that first chill that lets us know fall and then winter are just around the corner.

"How'd you sleep?" my mom asks, pulling another mug from the cupboard.

"Really well, actually. I didn't hear a peep out of Louisa until six thirty-five. So I got like nine hours of sleep."

"Oh wow, that's amazing," my mom says, passing me a cup of steaming-hot coffee and scooping Louisa into her arms in a fluid exchange. I sip the coffee gratefully and stare at Lulu. "She's just so amazing," I say. Louisa whines and struggles desperately to reach the iPad on the kitchen island. Later, my dad sets up the checkerboard in the library as I hold onto Louisa's hands and walk with her in a zigzagging pattern of a drunken sailor around the room. "You guys, look!" I say as she twists her feet and stumbles. "Look how close she is to walking!"

My mom and I bring Louisa to Scratch to stock up on home-made granola and rosé. The bakery is warm and bustling. The smell of croissants and freshly baked bagels hits us as we walk through the creaky wooden door.

"Look at those blue eyes! And that beautiful skin! What a lucky girl," one of the young employees says. I follow her eyes down to my own pale white arm and laugh. "Her father is Argentinian."

"Wow, that's the way to do it!" The employee laughs. "Good for you," she says with a wink. My stomach drops "Well, actually," I start. And then I stop. "Yes," I say with a small smile. "She's a very lucky girl."

Seb wakes up around 10:00 A.M., and it feels like a whole new day is starting as he trudges into the family room, rubbing his eyes. "Hey, guys, what's up? What's the plan for today?"

When I heard the crunch of Nat's tires a few days ago, announcing their arrival, I leaped up from the couch and ran out the front door. I stopped short for a moment, unsure what I would feel, seeing Seb for the first time since it all happened. And then he stepped out of the car and it was Seb. It was just Seb. We hugged, and I said, "You have an adult nose now?" and he grinned proudly. "I know. My mom says my features have developed literally overnight into 'man' features."

"We were thinking Ferry Beach?" I say, suggesting Seb's favorite beach, the one where he spends hours searching for hermit crabs.

When we get to the beach I ask Seb if he wants to come for a walk with me, and he says sure, shyly; he can sense that this isn't just a walk.

"I wanted to talk to you about a couple things," I start.

"I know, I know," Seb breathes out. "I was expecting this."

"Bear with me." I laugh. "I promise it'll be quick. I just want you to know that if you ever want to talk to me about what happened, or ask me any questions, you can. Anything. Anytime."

"Oh yeah, I know that," Seb says. "I've talked to my mom a lot."

"That's good. I'm really glad you guys are so close. It's important to me that you understand, though, that no one saw this coming. It wasn't like there were big, hidden adult secrets that you didn't know about all along. It was a shock to everyone." I awkwardly weave my way through what I'm trying to tell Seb. I don't want him to question his own perception of reality because of what happened.

"Yeah, yeah, I know." Seb nods.

"And I have a question for you." I take a deep breath. "I know the circumstances were a little different, but how has it been for you, growing up without your parents together?"

Seb looks up at me sharply, and I brace myself for the answer and for what his answer will mean for Lulu. I know that he is going to tell me that it was hard, that he always felt different from other kids. His face breaks into a smile. "Are you kidding me? My parents splitting was the best thing to ever happen to me. My mom and I talk about it all the time. How much we love our life together."

"Really?" I say. "Seriously?"

"God yes." He kicks the water as it laps around our feet. "I mean, I love my dad." His eyes drop, and he looks embarrassed. I want to hug him and say, "It's OK, you can love your dad, it's OK," but I just smile instead, and he continues. "But my mom and I are best friends, and we have such an awesome, cozy life together."

I let the wind blow away the tears forming.

"Is that it?" he says. "Can I hunt for hermit crabs now?"

———

THAT night I sprinkle warm water over Louisa's body with a toy watering can as she sits in the kitchen sink, and I compose a letter in my head:

> Louisa. Louisa. I find myself saying your name over and over again. Running my tongue against the syllables. I have never said a sweeter word. I look at you and I realize something. The part of me that I thought Marco ripped out? That I thought was missing, the void that could never be filled again? There was never a void. There was never a hole. Marco never took anything away from me because I was always whole to begin with. And that is what I am going to teach you, my love. You were born whole. Just look at you.
>
> I remember being in the hospital with you those first nights. You screamed and screamed, all night, so loudly that eventually a nurse poked her head into the room.
>
> "Everything OK in here?" she said with a worried look on her face.
>
> "I don't know what to do," I said, and then broke down in tears. Marco had left hours before, saying he had to

work, tie up some loose ends. A couple of hours turned into six hours and then it was 2:00 a.m. Nothing would stop your screaming. I put you on my breast, squeezing my eyes shut as your gums clamped down on my nipple like a trash compactor. I rocked you. I sang. I walked around and around the tiny room, bouncing and swaying. I waited for the love to come. I waited for it to course through my veins, that instinctive motherly love that would make the screaming and the pain all "worth it." Instead, panic flooded my body. What I really wanted to say to the nurse was, "I don't think I can do this. I'm so terribly sorry, but I need to go back in time. Please let me go back." Instead, I asked her to show me how to do a proper swaddle. She wrapped you up, swiftly and tightly, and you slept for the next five hours. You were sleeping when Marco walked back into the room at 2:45 a.m.

When we brought you home, I thought the panic would subside and the love would trickle in, slowly taking its place. But the panic grew. Unfocused and intense, I couldn't even pinpoint exactly what was so terrifying, I only knew that I needed to rip through my skin and flee, leaving the empty shell of my body there to deal with you and the new life that stretched before me. When I found the e-mail, suddenly I had so much else to worry about that the panic, the hormones, the fear, and you, my love, all faded into the background. I told myself, and others, that you were a blur for months because of what Marco did. When people asked me how motherhood was treating me, I shook my head and said with a wry laugh, "I honestly don't even remember much from Louisa's first months of life," and the reply would always come quickly, "Of course not, you were traumatized, but thank God you had your love for Louisa to carry you through. What a blessing." And I would nod, conceding that Marco had stolen those months from me and you. The golden excuse. But the truth is, I didn't fall in love with you all at once, like I did with your father. Here's the thing: I fell in love with Marco before I really knew him. It was a whimsical, stomach-churning, light-headed love. I fell in love with you bit by bit. I fell in love with your soft golden hair. I fell in love with your dimpled arms. I fell in love with the light in your eyes. I fell in love with the big gummy smile that fills your face 99 percent of the time. I fell in love with the crumpled frown followed by an earth-shattering scream when you topple over, more scared than hurt. I fell in love with the sharp, short, high-pitched shrieks and the low, rumbling lion roar. And once the tiny sapling of love took root, it began to grow. I realize now that it wasn't that I didn't love you; it was that I didn't recognize that I was falling in love with you slowly, in a way that was more pure, more profound, and more real than anything I had ever experienced before.

Lulu stands up in the tub, breaking me out of my thoughts. I wrap my arm around her slick body and lower her back into a sitting position. She furrows her brow, pushes back into a stand, and squawks gleefully. "Gah, Lu!" I grab her wrist right as her feet slide out from under her. "OK, tubby time is over. Tubby time ends early when you insist on standing," I tell her, and wrap her up in the towel waiting beside the sink. She opens and closes her mouth like a fish and stares at me from her towel hood. I lay her down on top of her pajamas, and she squiggles and struggles with one last burst of energy. "Ha! Done!" I cry victoriously as I do the last snap. My parents each kiss her good night, and "Love you, Lulu" follows us up the stairs. As she lays against me drinking her bottle, I think about how much I loved Marco and how sad I am that I don't have a husband anymore, but how I would rather live without a husband than live a life built on lies. This life, the one with me and Louisa, feels real in a way I hadn't known life could. I am happy.

Louisa finishes her bottle, and I turn her limp, milk-drunk body over and pat her on the back.

"Good night, animals," I say to the mobile as we pass. *"Un, deux, trois, quatre, cinq,"* I count the stars as I lower her into the crib. "Sleep well, my love. I'll see you in the morning," I whisper into her hair. And then I add, "I love you so."

Acknowledgments

EVERY achievement is comprised of a million, billion tiny moments/words/actions gifted to us (though it may not seem like a gift at the time) from other people. This memoir particularly so. And so I would like to thank:

My fearless, dynamic literary agent, Myrsini Stephanides, for taking a chance and rescuing me from the slush pile.

My ridiculously smart and intuitive editor for so gracefully easing me into making edits that strengthened this book and for being my voice in the sometimes scary world of publishing.

My writing consultant, Suzanne Kingsbury, who gave me the courage to embark on this journey.

Lynsey and all the sugarpunks—you have been my sisters and support system for twenty years. Thank you for sitting with me in the darkness until I could see the light.

My soul sister, Aga, for being nocturnal and always responding to my late-night texts.

My parents, words cannot . . . See? I just tried to write something and erased it four times. Without you two, this book, and everything else, would not exist. Thank you for saving us.

Lastly, to the reader—I am with you.